Myrtle Allen's Cooking at
BALLYMALOE HOUSE

Myrtle Allen's Cooking at

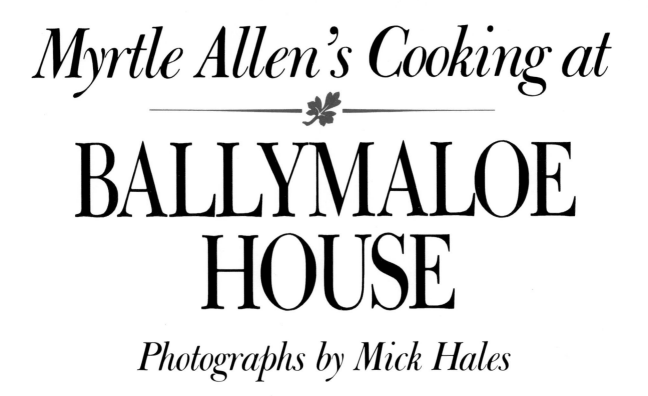

BALLYMALOE HOUSE

Photographs by Mick Hales

Stewart, Tabori & Chang
New York

For my granddaughters—
Lydia, Fawn, Emily, Caragh, Roisin,
Corinne, Maxine, Brigid, and Rosaleen

Published in 1990 by
Stewart, Tabori & Chang, Inc.
575 Broadway, New York, New York 10012

Text copyright © 1990 Myrtle Allen
Photographs copyright © 1990 Mick Hales
Map by Guenter Vollath

Library of Congress Cataloging-in-Publication Data
Allen, Myrtle, 1924–
   [Cooking at Ballymaloe House]
   Myrtle Allen's cooking at Ballymaloe House / photographs by Mick
Hales.
      p.   cm.
   ISBN 1-55670-158-6 : $29.95
   1. Cookery, Irish.   2. Ballymaloe House (Restaurant)   I. Title.
II. Title: Cooking at Ballymaloe House.
TX717.5.A45   1990
641.59415—dc20   90-34420
                                                          CIP

Distributed in the U.S. by Workman Publishing,
708 Broadway, New York, New York 10003
Distributed in Canada by Canadian Manda Group,
P.O. Box 920 Station U, Toronto, Ontario M8Z 5P9
Distributed in all other territories by Little,
Brown and Company, International Division, 34 Beacon Street,
Boston, Massachusetts 02108

Printed in Japan
10 9 8 7 6 5 4 3 2 1

CONTENTS

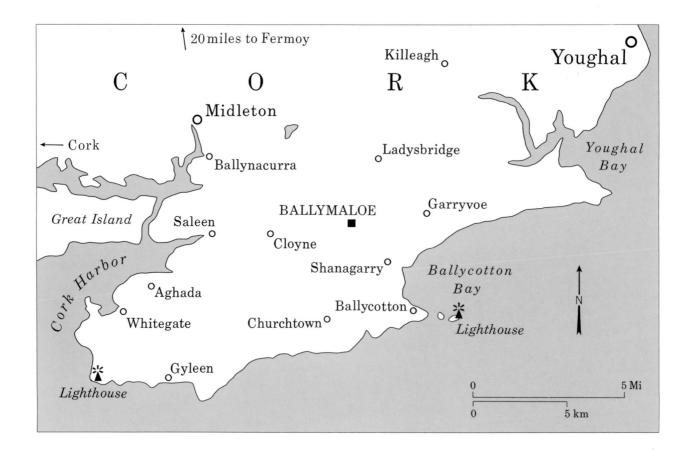

20 miles to Fermoy

C O R K

Killeagh

Youghal

Midleton

← Cork

Ballynacurra

Ladysbridge

Youghal Bay

Great Island

BALLYMALOE ■

Garryvoe

Saleen

Cloyne

Shanagarry

Cork Harbor

Aghada

Churchtown

Ballycotton

Ballycotton Bay

N

Whitegate

Gyleen

Ballycotton

Lighthouse

Lighthouse

0   5 Mi

0   5 km

Foreword

Myrtle Allen's Ballymaloe House evokes a time and place—a real memory for some of us, a dream for others—when summer meant freshly squeezed lemonade and blackberry sorbet; when breakfast was a full meal, complete with stoneground oatmeal, warm scones, and fresh orange juice; and when Christmas preparations were begun months in advance with the baking of plum pudding. This tranquil, satisfying pattern of living still exists at Ballymaloe House in southwestern Ireland. Here, Myrtle Allen presides over a kitchen that prepares seasonal dishes highlighting the incomparable local produce, and a small luxurious hotel where every detail is attended to for the comfort of her guests.

Ballymaloe House itself is large and commanding without being intimidating or overwhelming. Inside, the rooms are welcoming: fresh flowers from the garden in small pots give off a spicy fragrance; the sheets are cotton and ironed; the towels are oversized. There is no television, no radio, no lock on the door, no sound but the gentle rain on the windowpane.

It soon becomes apparent, however, that the kitchen is the center of this house. Remarkable food comes from the kitchen in abundance, starting with the delicious breakfast coffee made from Myrtle's own selection of beans. All the breads—including the famous Ballymaloe Brown Bread—are baked each morning, and as needed throughout the day.

The ingredients available in this part of Ireland are among the finest in the world. The butter is rich and full of flavor; the cream is thick and sweet; the strawberries are juicy and ripe; the fish is caught and brought immediately from the bay to Myrtle Allen's kitchen door. Her standards are demanding, and she never stops looking for the best. If the almonds aren't fresh enough, the almond tartlets aren't made that night, and a search is begun the next day to discover what might be the problem or perhaps to urge the supplier to look for a better source.

It is Myrtle Allen's attention to detail and devotion to quality that make guests at Ballymaloe feel so well cared for. For those who have not had the opportunity to stay at the house and enjoy the wonderful food, we hope that *Myrtle Allen's Cooking at Ballymaloe House* will serve as a pleasant introduction to her cooking. The book has been edited to reflect American measurements and ingredients, but Myrtle Allen's stories about the recipes and the Irish legends of her girlhood remain in her own voice.

The Editors

Introduction

I have been a recipe collector ever since I was very young. I look everywhere for a find, the magic formula that will work for me, with my ingredients and my knowledge of how to handle them according to my experience and the purpose of the moment. Cooking comes down to a sort of alchemy, its result an elixir, for suddenly here on one's table for family and friends is a new delicious concoction, a pleasure for everyone.

So this book is really a sample from my collection. The recipes come from many different sources: from old, handwritten, family cookery books; from friends; and from books, magazines, and manuals. A gem can just as easily turn up in a cheap little book of local ladies' home-cooking secrets collected for charity as in the works of the great and famous writers and chefs. Some recipes have been worked out painfully, with many failures along the way. I do, however, owe a great debt to some prominent people, particularly to Jane Grigson; also to Simone Beck, formerly of L'Ecole Trois Gourmands in Paris; and to the late Rosemary Hume of the Cordon Bleu School in London. From these three sources I learned many of my basic techniques.

Here and there you will find that my instructions are not relevant to contemporary conditions of living, such as a modern apartment. For instance, "leave in a cool larder" will not be possible for many readers. If this is the authentic and best way to handle a certain dish, however, I have left it in the recipe instructions, along with more modern alternatives.

The main part of my cooking experience has been gained in Ballymaloe, a big house on a 400-acre farm, where I have lived since 1947. Cooking in a farmhouse usually means that one has very fresh produce at hand and a hungry tableful of helpers and family waiting to be fed. With no easy access to shops and markets and crops coming in in gluts, one soon learns every possible way of cooking whatever cannot be profitably sold. We loved to entertain our friends as well. So, in 1964, I felt that I had enough experience to open part of our house as a restaurant. It grew and grew, rooms were opened for overnight stays, and this soon became one of the main lines in our farming business.

Our children with their husbands and wives came to help run the house, the farm, and new satellite businesses. Grandchildren help as well, sometimes.

Cutting flowers and herbs in the walled garden at Ballymaloe.

My tables are many now. There are two restaurants and twenty-odd chefs working with Paddy and Billy in my kitchen. My daughter-in-law Darina, who trained with me and then married my elder son, operates the Ballymaloe Cooking School nearby. Her brother, Rory O'Connell, is also presently working with me. Some people call him the Sorcerer's Apprentice, especially when I say, "How did Rory do *that*?" He carries forward, and beyond, much of my work.

I conclude by wishing that the reader will discover some gem in this collection.

Myrtle Allen
Ballymaloe House
Shanagarry, 1990

SOUPS AND STARTERS

Tomato Juice

— ❧ —

After many experiments to get a good tomato juice, I decided that nothing tasted better than the juice left from a tomato salad. I tried to adapt it by guessing how much seasoning, herbs, and French dressing I would put over some tomatoes, and then I puréed the lot. It was like playing tennis. If you have a good eye and concentrate on your shot you get a good result. If somebody talked to me in the middle, I would do something awful like putting in two lots of vinegar. In the end, I came up with this recipe.

The tomatoes must be almost at that point of ripeness when the skin will peel off easily without one's first having to scald them.

2½	cups (about 1 pound) peeled and coarsely chopped very ripe tomatoes
1	scallion including the green part, cut into 1-inch pieces
3	fresh basil or mint leaves or 1 sprig of fresh tarragon
2	teaspoons white-wine vinegar
1	tablespoon olive oil
1	teaspoon salt
1	teaspoon sugar
¼	teaspoon coarsely ground black pepper

In a food processor or blender purée the tomatoes, scallion, basil, vinegar, oil, salt, sugar, and pepper until smooth. Strain the mixture through a sieve into a bowl, stir in ½ cup water, and chill the juice for up to 12 hours.

Yield: about 3 cups

Note: Leftover Tomato Juice can be boiled down until thickened to use as a tomato sauce.

VARIATION

Tomato Ring

Make the preceding Tomato Juice omitting the oil and the water. Soften 1½ packages unflavored gelatin in ¼ cup water, heat the mixture over low heat, stirring, until the gelatin is dissolved, and stir it into the tomato juice. Pour into a 3-cup lightly oiled ring mold and chill for at least 4 hours, or until set. Unmold onto a lettuce-lined platter and fill the center with crab meat mixed with mayonnaise and a little grated onion.

The most *delicious filling for a tomato ring is crab mayonnaise, a wonderful combination of tastes and textures.*

Persian Cocktail

The effect of climate on food fascinates me. It isn't just whether you have a gooseberry bush or a banana tree in the back garden; it is the moisture, the soil, herbs, winds, and indigenous bacteria, which affect not only the kind but also the quality of food in different places.

I loathed yogurt until I bought a plastic bagful from a nomad in the mountains northwest of Teheran. This was just something different again. All the learned men and expensive laboratories of northwestern Europe cannot reproduce this type of yogurt. No wonder. What it takes is a wild and tough man, backed by a herd of goats, a tribe of relations, a few earthenware jars, and a vast area of barren mountainside alternately roasting and freezing.

The Iranians know what they have got. They eat and drink it in every conceivable way. The best I could do when I got home was to take a Persian idea and adapt it to Irish materials. This concoction is not Persian and certainly not Irish. It is good in its own right for starting a gentle summer dinner. Use within twenty-four hours.

1   garlic clove
1   teaspoon salt
½   pound ripe tomatoes, peeled and chopped coarse
2   cups plain yogurt
2   teaspoons finely chopped fresh mint leaves plus 4 to 5 whole mint leaves for garnish

Peel and mash the garlic with the salt to make a paste. In a food processor or blender purée the garlic mixture with the tomatoes. Strain through a sieve into a bowl, if desired. Stir in the yogurt and mint and chill for at least 30 minutes. Transfer to long-stemmed wineglasses and top each serving with a mint leaf.

Yield: 4 to 5 servings

Cool starters for a summer dinner—Persian Cocktail, Tomato Juice, and Grapefruit and Lovage Cocktail.

Grapefruit, Lovage, and Cucumber Salad

———— ❧ ————

Grapes, melons, grapefruits, oranges, and tomatoes combine to make a good juicy base for a fruit first course.

Chopped radish, celery, cucumber, watercress stalks, the crisp white top of a cauliflower or the dark purple bud of purple sprouting broccoli—all add a crunchy texture. Chopped bell peppers and scallions are particularly good with tomatoes.

Fresh mint, dill, thyme, lovage, and basil, if you can get them, give aroma and flavor. Never use too much, though. Treat herbs with caution until you know them well.

1   grapefruit, peeled, halved, and sectioned, discarding the membranes
¼   cucumber, peeled, halved lengthwise, seeded, and sliced thin crosswise
½   lovage leaf, crushed, plus 2 whole leaves

In a bowl combine the grapefruit, cucumber, and crushed lovage leaf. Chill for at least 1 hour or up to 12 hours. Remove and discard the crushed leaf and let the mixture return to room temperature.

Put 1 whole lovage leaf on each of 2 small plates or in each of 2 stemmed glasses. Divide the grapefruit mixture between the plates or glasses, partly covering the leaves.

Yield: 2 servings

French Peasant Soup

———— ❧ ————

This recipe is based on a French country soup, and it is very popular in our restaurant. I sometimes serve it when I go abroad to cook for an Irish occasion or to "cook an Irish meal," but I have to change the name. We often served it in my Paris restaurant, where it was called Connemara Broth, while in Ballymaloe the same soup was selling as French Peasant Soup. It's all in a name!

2 ounces lean salt pork, diced (about ½ cup)
1 onion, chopped (about ½ cup)
1 potato (about 6 ounces), peeled and diced (about 1 cup)
1 garlic clove, minced
¾ cup shredded cabbage (preferably savoy)
1½ cups chopped peeled tomatoes
3 cups chicken, beef, or vegetable stock or canned broth
1 teaspoon sugar

In a heavy 3-quart saucepan cook the salt pork over moderate heat until it is golden brown and the fat is rendered. Remove the pork with a slotted spoon and reserve it. Add the onion, potato, and garlic to the fat and toss them for 1 minute, or until they are coated. Reduce the heat to low and sweat the vegetables, covered, for 10 minutes, or until they are somewhat softened.

Add the cabbage, tomatoes, stock, sugar, and salt and pepper to taste. Simmer the mixture, covered, for about 10 minutes, or until the cabbage is just tender. Return the reserved salt pork to the pan and simmer the soup for 1 minute. Taste and adjust the seasonings.

Yield: about 6 cups, serving 4

Onions growing with parsley and spinach in the walled garden at Ballymaloe.

Lettuce and Mint Soup

— ❧ —

This is one of the nicest soups we make in late spring, using fresh mint and the outside leaves, or shot heads, of lettuce. Do not overcook the vegetables or they will lose their flavor.

½ stick (¼ cup) unsalted butter
1 cup chopped onion
1 potato (about 6 ounces), peeled and chopped coarse (about 1 cup)
5 cups chicken stock or canned chicken broth
1 teaspoon salt (optional)
¼ teaspoon freshly ground black pepper
3 cups lightly packed chopped lettuce leaves
1 tablespoon chopped fresh mint
1 tablespoon heavy cream (optional)

Melt the butter in a heavy 3-quart saucepan over moderate heat, add the onion and potato, and toss them in the butter for about 1 minute. Reduce the heat to low and sweat the vegetables, covered, for about 10 minutes, or until they are somewhat softened. Add the stock, salt (omit if using canned broth), and pepper and simmer the mixture, covered, for about 10 minutes. Add the lettuce and simmer, uncovered, for 5 to 6 minutes, or until all the vegetables are softened.

Purée the soup in batches in a food processor or blender. Taste and adjust the seasonings. Just before serving stir in the mint and cream.

Yield: about 8 cups, serving 6

Cold Cucumber Soup

— ❧ —

There are several versions of this well-tempered dish. It is easy to make, delicious to eat, and keeps for days. Try setting it in a ring mold with gelatin (see Variation).

2 cucumbers (about 1 pound total) or 1 large seedless cucumber
2 cups light cream or half-and-half
1 cup plain yogurt
3 tablespoons Tarragon Vinegar (page 26)
1 garlic clove, minced
3 tablespoons finely chopped gherkins (small firm, sweet pickles)
¼ cup finely chopped fresh mint leaves

Peel, seed, and grate the cucumber. In a bowl stir together the grated cucumber, cream, yogurt, vinegar, garlic, gherkins, and salt and pepper to taste. Chill the soup for about 1 hour, then serve with some of the mint stirred in and the remainder sprinkled on top.

Yield: about 4½ cups

VARIATION

Cucumber Ring

In a small saucepan soften 1 package unflavored gelatin in 1 tablespoon cold water and dissolve the gelatin over low heat, stirring. Blend the dissolved gelatin into 2 to 2½ cups cold soup and pour into a 3-cup ring mold or 3 to 4 individual ring molds. Chill for at least 4 hours, or until set.

Fill the center with a bouquet of green leaves, such as a mixed bunch of pale lettuce leaves and watercress sprigs as well as scallions, and long sticks of cucumber. Pass French dressing separately.

Quick Tomato Soup

Ripeness is everything in a good tomato soup or purée. Unless the fruit is dark red, don't use it. To ripen the fruit put it in a warm place; or, better still, shop around for overripe fruit. You might get them cheap.

2   tablespoons unsalted butter
3   tablespoons chopped onion
1   pound ripe tomatoes, peeled and chopped
1   tablespoon chopped fresh herbs such as thyme, tarragon, mint, or basil
½   teaspoon sugar
3   cups chicken stock or canned chicken broth
2   tablespoons heavy cream (optional)

Melt the butter in a heavy 3-quart, non-reactive saucepan over low heat and cook the onion in it for about 3 minutes, or until softened. Add the tomatoes, herbs, sugar, and salt (omit if using canned broth) and pepper to taste and simmer, covered, for 8 minutes.

Add the stock and simmer the soup for 5 minutes. Taste and adjust the seasonings. Stir in the cream.

Yield: about 5 cups, serving 3 to 4

Overleaf: Golfing at Ballymaloe.

Tartare Sauce

❧

This is an accompaniment to any plain broiled fish but is especially good with fried fish using the fish batter on page 46.

1   *hard-boiled extra-large egg, separated, the white chopped*
1   *raw extra-large egg at room temperature, separated, reserving the white for another use*
1   *tablespoon white-wine or malt vinegar*
¾   *cup olive oil*
1   *teaspoon chopped drained bottled capers*
1   *teaspoon chopped gherkins (small firm, sweet pickles)*
1   *tablespoon chopped fresh chives or scallion greens*

In a small bowl mash the hard-boiled egg yolk and whisk in the raw egg yolk and the vinegar. Add the oil, whisking, drop by drop at first and then in a very thin stream as the sauce emulsifies. Stir in the capers, gherkins, chives, hard-boiled egg white, and salt and pepper to taste.

The sauce keeps, covered and chilled, for 3 days.

Yield: about 1 cup

Billy's French Dressing

❧

Sometimes our chef Billy has his moments. One time I noticed an amazingly good French dressing coming up from the kitchen. I went down to investigate. As he stuffed greens and seasonings into the blender, I rushed for a pen and paper to record what was going on.

¼   *cup mild wine vinegar*
1   *teaspoon Dijon-style mustard*
1   *teaspoon salt*
¼   *teaspoon freshly ground black pepper*
1   *large garlic clove, minced*
1   *scallion, chopped coarse*
1   *sprig of parsley*
1   *sprig of watercress*
¾   *cup vegetable or olive oil or a combination*

In a food processor or blender purée all the ingredients. The dressing keeps, covered and chilled, for 24 hours. Return to room temperature before using.

Yield: about 1 cup

Lydia's Cream Dressing

———— ❧ ————

Oil was not considered as a food in the average Irish household during the first half of the century. There was always a small glass bottle of rancid olive oil in our house, but it was kept in the medicine cupboard and used for sunburns. Cream dressings were served with salads. The Traditional Salad (page 91) was and still is standard fare for Sunday evening suppers, accompanying cold meat, usually left over from the midday joint. No dressing goes better with it than Lydia Strangman's. Sister of my husband's elderly farming partner, she was an unmarried Quaker lady of strict principles, who spent her life painting and making a beautiful garden.

It is interesting to note the similarity of this Irish dressing to mayonnaise: Cream replaces olive oil in a country where olives cannot grow; hard-boiled egg yolk replaces raw; but the seasonings are the same.

2   hard-boiled extra-large eggs, separated
1   tablespoon light brown sugar
¼   teaspoon salt
¼   teaspoon dry English mustard
2   teaspoons malt vinegar
5   tablespoons heavy cream

Sieve the egg yolks and chop the whites. In a bowl combine the sieved yolks with the brown sugar, salt, and mustard. Stir in the vinegar and cream. (Reserve the chopped whites for sprinkling over the salad.)

The dressing keeps, covered and chilled, for 24 hours.

Yield: about ½ cup

Tarragon Vinegar

If you grow tarragon in summer, it is well worth picking and preserving it for winter use. It is most abundant just before flowering, so this is the best time to collect surplus growth.

2 cups fresh tarragon leaves
3 cups malt or white-wine vinegar

Crush the tarragon leaves in your hands and put them in bottles. Fill the bottles with the vinegar and cover tightly. Let the vinegar stand in a cool dark place for at least 2 weeks before using.

Yield: about 3 cups

Garlic Mayonnaise

This is a savory variation on our basic mayonnaise. At Ballymaloe it is used as an accompaniment to cold roast beef and fish. Use as much garlic as your taste and needs dictate.

2 extra-large egg yolks at room temperature
1 tablespoon white-wine vinegar
1 to 4 garlic cloves, crushed with ¼ teaspoon salt to make a paste
⅛ teaspoon dry English mustard or ¼ teaspoon Dijon-style
1 cup vegetable or olive oil
1 tablespoon minced fresh parsley leaves

In a small bowl whisk the yolks with 1½ teaspoons of the vinegar, the garlic paste, and mustard. Whisk in the oil, at first by droplets and then in a very thin stream as the sauce emulsifies. When about ¾ cup of the oil has been added and the sauce becomes very thick, whisk in the remaining 1½ teaspoons vinegar. Whisk in the remaining ¼ cup oil and fold in the parsley.

The mayonnaise keeps, covered and chilled, for 2 days.

Yield: about 1 cup

Mint Sauce

---- ❧ ----

This is a very simple version of a classic mint sauce that is served with roast lamb.

3½   tablespoons finely chopped fresh mint leaves
1½   tablespoons sugar
2   tablespoons white-wine vinegar

In a small bowl combine the mint and sugar. Add 7 tablespoons boiling water and the vinegar and let the sauce infuse for 5 to 10 minutes, or until it is the desired strength. Taste and add up to 2 tablespoons additional boiling water if the sauce seems too strong.

Yield: about ½ cup

Tomato Chutney

---- ❧ ----

This chutney keeps for weeks in the refrigerator. If you have lots of ripe tomatoes, make it in larger quantities and put it up in canning jars. Use the chutney as a condiment or as part of Ballymaloe Cheese Fondue (page 30).

⅔   cup granulated sugar
1   teaspoon salt
½   teaspoon whole mustard seeds
¼   teaspoon freshly ground pepper
½   cup red wine vinegar
½   cup white wine or white cider vinegar
1   pound ripe tomatoes, peeled and coarsely chopped
1   bunch scallions, chopped including green parts (about 1 cup)

In a non-reactive saucepan, combine the sugar, salt, mustard seed, and pepper. Stir in both vinegars and bring to a boil. Add the tomatoes and scallions. Simmer gently, uncovered, for about 1 hour, or until the mixture has thickened to a liquid jam consistency.

Cool and refrigerate for up to several weeks.

Yield: about 2 cups

PATES, CHEESES, AND EGGS

Ballymaloe Cheese Fondue

❧

There are plenty of records that refer to cheesemaking in Ireland, from the earliest times to the late seventeenth century, at which point cheese production declined until the art of making it was forgotten—nobody knows exactly why. Meanwhile, buttermaking increased, and by the nineteenth century Ireland had a great butter export trade.

In the 1930s farmers' co-operative dairies started to make cheese again, and for the last forty-odd years they have been turning out a delicious Cheddar-type cheese in big rolls. In the seventies and eighties, with an EEC levy on milk production, farmhouse cheesemakers started to emerge with quite wonderful products.

This fondue is a Ballymaloe specialty. It is quite unlike a Swiss fondue, although it is served in the same way. Use a mild Cheddar or similar cheese that melts easily.

2 tablespoons dry white wine
1 small garlic clove, minced
1 tablespoon Tomato Chutney (page 27)
2 cups (about ½ pound) grated medium or mild Cheddar
1 tablespoon chopped fresh parsley leaves
Large cubes of French bread or white bread, toasted lightly

Combine all the ingredients except the parsley and bread in the top of a double boiler set over simmering water or in a fondue pot over very low heat and stir until the cheese is melted and smooth. Stir in the parsley.

Serve immediately with the bread cubes for dipping.

Yield: 2 main-course servings

Soft, hard, blue, goat's, and sheep's cheeses have re-emerged in Ireland after a lapse of 300 years.

Dutch Cheese Croquettes

——— ❧ ———

We use local Irish Cheddar for this dish, but a good medium-sharp Cheddar that is not too dry is suitable.

FOR THE CROQUETTES
5 tablespoons unsalted butter
5 tablespoons all-purpose flour
2 cups milk
2 extra-large egg yolks, beaten
2 cups grated Cheddar
2 tablespoons snipped fresh chives

About ½ cup all-purpose flour
¼ teaspoon salt
⅛ teaspoon black pepper
1 extra-large egg, beaten with 1 tablespoon milk
1 cup unseasoned dry bread crumbs
Vegetable oil for deep-frying the croquettes

To make the croquettes, heat the butter in a heavy saucepan over moderately low heat. Whisk in the flour until smooth and then cook the *roux*, whisking, for 2 minutes. Slowly whisk in the milk, cook the mixture, stirring constantly, until it thickens and comes to a boil, and cook the sauce for 2 minutes more. In a bowl whisk about 1 cup of the sauce into the beaten yolks, then turn the mixture into the pan and cook over low heat, stirring, for about 2 minutes, or until very thick. (Do not let the mixture boil.) Over very low heat stir in the cheese by handfuls, stirring until each handful melts before adding another, and then stir in the chives. Scrape the mixture into a shallow pan and chill it for at least 4 hours or overnight (it should be very firm).

Combine the flour, salt, and pepper in a shallow dish and put the egg mixture and bread crumbs in separate dishes. Form the chilled mixture into 1- to 1½-inch balls. Dip the croquettes, one at a time, first into the seasoned flour, then into the beaten egg, and finally into the unseasoned bread crumbs, coating them completely. Arrange in a single layer in a shallow pan and chill for at least 1 hour or up to 4 hours, or until very firm.

Heat at least 2 inches of vegetable oil to 370° F. in a deep-fryer or deep saucepan. Fry the croquettes, a few at a time, for 3 to 4 minutes, or until rich golden brown. Drain on paper towels and serve hot.

Yield: about 16 croquettes

Eggs with Hot Herbed Mayonnaise

❦

Th ese soft-boiled eggs, nicely sauced and set on a crouton, make a light lunch or supper dish or a starter for dinner.

FOR THE HERBED MAYONNAISE

1	extra-large egg, soft-boiled and separated
2	teaspoons fresh lemon juice
½	cup vegetable or olive oil
2½	teaspoons minced shallots or chives
2½	teaspoons chopped fresh herbs such as thyme and tarragon
¼	teaspoon Dijon-style mustard
¼	teaspoon salt
3	to 4 tablespoons chicken stock or canned chicken broth

6	extra-large eggs
3	large slices of firm white bread
1	to 2 tablespoons unsalted butter or oil

To make the mayonnaise, in the top of a double boiler set over hot water whisk the soft-boiled yolk with the lemon juice. Whisk in the oil by droplets at first and then, after the mayonnaise has begun to emulsify, in a thin stream. Stir in the shallots, herbs, mustard, salt, and enough of the stock to thin the mayonnaise to a sauce-like consistency. Chop the egg white and stir it into the mayonnaise. Keep warm in the pan over warm water.

Cut 6 ovals slightly larger than the eggs from the bread slices, sauté them in the butter or oil until golden brown, and transfer the croutons to paper towels to drain. Lower the eggs gently into a saucepan of simmering water to cover and simmer them gently for 4 minutes. Peel the eggs and set each on a crouton. Spoon the warm sauce over the eggs.

Yield: 3 main-course or 6 first-course servings

Chicken Liver Pâté

In the 1960s the most prestigious kitchen in Ireland was that of the Russell Hotel in Dublin, under Chef Roland. Many of our best chefs today spent some time training under him.

One day I decided to ask the manager if my eldest daughter, Wendy, would be accepted in the kitchen for a few months. He was doubtful. A girl had never entered their kitchen (except to clean up after the men); however, he would ask the chef. The message came back that in fact he would love to have a girl in the kitchen, particularly as she had already learned to cook in France. So off she went. Wendy brought home a great many good tips. One saying of Mr. Roland was "If you cannot get your dish right, just add more butter or cream."

When I started to make Chicken Liver Pâté, I followed this advice—using plenty of butter in this case. It is best served at room temperature; if served too cold, it's brittle; if served too warm, it's overly soft.

1   stick (½ cup) unsalted butter, softened, plus additional, melted, for the topping (optional)
¼   pound chicken livers
1   tablespoon brandy
1   large garlic clove, minced
1   teaspoon minced fresh thyme

In a skillet melt 2 tablespoons of the butter over moderately high heat until the foam subsides and in it sauté the chicken livers, stirring often, for 5 to 7 minutes, or until cooked through. Force the cooked livers through a coarse sieve into a bowl and discard the tough fibers. Add the brandy to the skillet, heat it over moderate heat, scraping up the browned bits, and beat it into the sieved livers with the remaining 6 tablespoons softened butter, garlic, and thyme. Taste and season with salt and pepper.

Transfer the pâté to a 1-cup ramekin and either serve it, for spreading, immediately or chill it, covered with plastic wrap, for at least 1 hour and up to 24 hours. Bring the pâté to room temperature before serving. The pâté keeps, covered with ⅛ inch melted butter and chilled, for 3 days.

Yield: about ⅔ cup

Danish Liver Pâté

Many years ago, when we started a herd of Jerseys, we went on an unsuccessful expedition to Denmark. We wanted to buy a Danish Jersey bull to increase the butterfat content of our milk.

It transpired, in the end, that we would not be permitted to import one of these fine Danish bulls, but we spent a pleasant week looking at their herds. We drank homemade wines in spotless farmhouse parlors; met sweet, flaxen-haired children; and thought that even their pigs had a quieter temperament than ours.

We did not come home quite empty-handed either. I returned with this recipe for Danish liver pâté, which we made whenever we killed a pig.

If you are using pork fat for this recipe, more salt is needed than when using bacon fat. It is essential to fry a little piece of the pâté and taste it before packing it into the loaf pans and baking it. Without sufficient salt the pâté is very bland and uninteresting. It is at its best when eaten still warm from the oven but can be stored for up to a week in the refrigerator.

1   pound 2 ounces pork liver
1   pound 2 ounces pork fat or bacon fat
2   onions chopped very fine
1   stick (½ cup) unsalted butter
1   cup flour
2   cups whole milk
A dash of paprika
6   large eggs, separated, the whites at room
    temperature

In a meat grinder grind fine the liver and fat and in a bowl combine them with the onion. In a saucepan melt the butter and whisk in the flour and milk. Add salt and pepper to taste. Stir in the meat mixture, paprika, and yolks, beaten lightly. In a bowl beat the whites until they hold stiff peaks and fold them into the mixture. Transfer the mixture to 2 loaf pans, approximately 8½ by 4½ by 2½ inches, set them in a roasting pan filled with enough water to reach halfway up the sides of the loaf pans, and bake the pâtés in a preheated 300°F. oven for about 2 hours, or until they are browned on top.

Yield: 30 servings as a first course; 10 to 12 servings as a main course

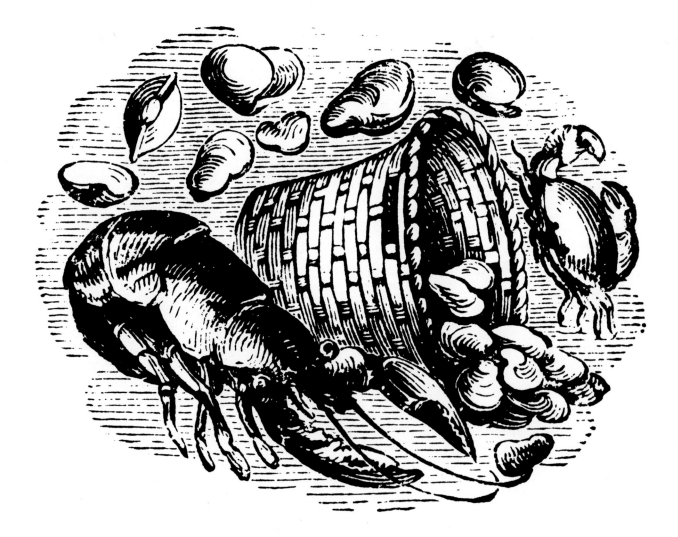

FISH AND SHELLFISH

Hot Buttered Oysters

———— ❧ ————

To open, or shuck, an oyster, place the oyster on a tea towel, flat side up. Wrap one hand in another cloth so that you do not get cut if the knife slips. Take your oyster knife in your other hand. (A chisel will have to do if you don't have an oyster knife.) Look for a chink or crevice in the shell at the narrow, hinged end. Insert the blade and press, turn, and lever upward. Use all your strength and keep at it—the shell will open. When it does, insert a clean knife and cut the oyster away from the top shell.

I know what to do with spoiled cauliflowers, soft tomatoes, old hens, and scraps of fat meat. I enjoy using what the world discards. My best find was for damaged cooking oysters. The following recipe makes a lovely supper dish. Cheer yourself up with this and a glass of chilled white wine, if you are all alone. It is also good for a small informal party of four to six people. Get them to help you with opening the oysters.

1   tablespoon unsalted butter
4   to 6 oysters, shucked (see above), reserving
    their liquid
1   slice of toast, buttered
1   lemon wedge

In a small skillet heat half the butter until it foams. Toss the oysters in the butter for about 1 minute, or until they're heated through. Spoon the oysters onto the toast. Pour the reserved oyster liquid into the skillet and bring it to a boil. Swirl in the remaining butter and pour the sauce over the oysters on the toast. Serve immediately with the lemon wedge.

Yield: 1 serving

In Ballycotton on a calm summer evening the pier is packed with buyers: the commercial men with vans, the hoteliers, and ordinary people hoping to find something for their supper.

Potted Crab

Potted fish or a fish pâté or mousse makes a wonderfully easy lunch or supper dish. Packed into tiny individual pots, a selection of any three makes a stunning dinner party starter. They are not suitable for picnics, unless packed in a chilled container, because the butter goes soft.

1   cup (about 5 ounces) fresh crab meat
1   stick (½ cup) unsalted butter, softened
1   tablespoon minced fresh parsley leaves
1   garlic clove, minced
¼   teaspoon freshly ground black pepper
1   tablespoon bottled tomato or mango chutney
Thin slices of whole-wheat bread as an
    accompaniment (optional)

Combine all ingredients in a bowl until blended well.

This dish may be served soon after preparation, but if you wish to keep it pack it into 1 large or several small crocks, cover the surface with a thin layer of melted butter, and chill the mixture. Serve the crab with the bread.

Yield: about 1½ cups

Smoked Mackerel Mousse

Try this recipe with other smoked fish; it is especially good with smoked salmon.

4   ounces boneless smoked mackerel
1   stick (½ cup) unsalted butter, ½ stick
    softened and the remaining ½ stick melted
    (optional)
½   teaspoon finely snipped fennel leaves
1   teaspoon fresh lemon juice
1   small garlic clove, minced
Thin slices of whole-wheat bread as an
    accompaniment (optional)

In a bowl blend the mackerel, softened butter, fennel leaves, lemon juice, and garlic. Pack the mixture into small crocks or a small loaf pan and chill it for 3 hours. The mousse keeps, covered with a thin layer of the melted butter and chilled, for 2 days. Serve the mousse with the bread.

Yield: about ¾ cup

Ripe lemons from Sicily complement food from Ballycotton: oysters, plaice, and shining mackerel fresh from the sea; cooked lobsters and crabs; and wild watercress.

Mussels in Mayonnaise

———— ❧ ————

To prepare mussels for cooking, begin by scrubbing them well. Each has a fibrous tuft, called the beard, protruding from the middle of the straight edge, which must be removed. When steaming them (see instructions below), remember that the longer they cook, the smaller and more leathery they become. They will be juicy and almost raw if you eat them at the first moment of opening. At this stage they are indeed the poor man's oyster. Spoon the mayonnaise over mussels in the half shell and serve with brown bread.

1   extra-large egg yolk
½   teaspoon vinegar
½   teaspoon fresh lemon juice
1   small garlic clove, minced
½   cup olive oil
About 2 dozen mussels, scrubbed and debearded

Whisk the egg yolk, vinegar, lemon juice, the garlic, and salt to taste in a small bowl. Whisk in the oil, at first by droplets and then in a very thin stream as the sauce emulsifies. The mayonnaise keeps, covered and chilled, for 2 days.

In a kettle steam the mussels over low heat in one or two layers in about 1 inch of water or white wine for 5 minutes, or until the shells open, and with a slotted spoon transfer them to a bowl. Reserve 3 tablespoons cooking liquid. Discard the top shell and loosen the mussels in their bottom shells. Arrange the mussels in the half shell on a platter.

Just before serving, stir the reserved cooking liquid into the mayonnaise (the sauce should be the consistency of thick cream). Spoon about 1½ teaspoons sauce over each mussel in the half shell.

Yield: about ¾ cup

42

Small boats anchored in Ballycotton's harbor.

Baked Rainbow Trout in Spinach Sauce

———— ❧ ————

I was invited to Brussels to cook during an Irish food fortnight at a big hotel there. Irish food, Irish cooking? Well, they'd had French, Chinese, Scandinavian, Italian, Russian, Indian, and American food and appeared to be bored by the lot. I'll swear they actually *needed* brown soda bread. Apple cakes made with Bramley's seedlings, good old Irish bacon and sausages, and Irish stew took on a new air of being rather special. This experience gave me the idea of opening an Irish restaurant in Paris. Our native dishes met with the same success as in Brussels, but, if I took Irish stew to France, I also brought home French sauces, such as the following spinach butter sauce for trout.

4   whole rainbow trout, boned (about ½ pound
    each) or eight ¼-pound trout fillets
2   tablespoons unsalted butter, cut into bits
    sprigs of fennel leaves

FOR THE SPINACH BUTTER SAUCE
¼   pound spinach leaves, washed well
1   cup heavy cream
10 tablespoons unsalted butter, cut into bits and
    softened
4   lemon wedges

On each of 4 large pieces of foil center 1 whole trout or 2 trout fillets. Dot the trout with the butter and sprinkle with salt and pepper to taste. Lay a fennel sprig over each fish. Completely enclose the fish in the foil, crumpling the edges to seal the packets. Bake the trout on a baking sheet in a preheated 375° F. oven for 20 to 30 minutes, or until they are just done.

While the trout is cooking, make the sauce: Steam the spinach in a little water for 2 minutes, or until it is wilted. Drain the spinach well in a sieve, pressing out excess liquid, and chop it. In a heavy saucepan boil the cream down to ¼ cup, watching carefully to prevent its burning. Whisk in the butter bit by bit over very low heat, adding more butter only when the previous bit has been incorporated. When the butter has all been incorporated and the sauce is thickened, stir in the chopped spinach and add salt and pepper to taste.

Unwrap the trout and divide it with the cooking juices among 4 plates. (If the sauce seems too thick, thin it with some of the juices.) Spoon the sauce over the trout and garnish with the lemon wedges.

Yield: 4 servings

Batter-Fried Fish Fillets

B atter-fried fish fillets have been so commercialized, people have forgotten how really good they can be if the batter is crisp, the fillets are fresh, and the frying fat is a sweet fresh dripping or a very good oil. The batter must be mixed and beaten thoroughly, or it will disintegrate when it is put into hot fat.

FOR THE BATTER
½   cup all-purpose flour
⅛   teaspoon salt
1   medium egg, beaten
1   tablespoon unsalted butter, melted
About ½ cup milk

2   pounds flat fish fillets, such as sole or other
    firm white fish
Oil for deep-frying the fish

To make the batter, stir the flour and salt together in a small bowl, make a well in the center, and stir in the egg, butter, and ¼ cup of the milk, gradually drawing the flour into the liquid until the batter is smooth. Add the remaining milk, a little at a time, until the batter coats the back of the spoon. Let the batter stand at least 15 minutes. The batter may be made 2 days in advance and kept covered and chilled. (The longer the batter stands, the thicker it will become; you may need to add more milk to restore the original consistency.)

Heat 2 to 3 inches of the oil to 370° F. in a kettle or deep saucepan. Pat the fish dry and dip them into the batter in batches, coating them completely and letting the excess drip off. Fry

Tommy Sliney, with his placid donkey, delivers freshly caught fish to the townspeople of Cloyne.

the fillets in batches, turning them carefully so that the coating is not disturbed, for 4 to 5 minutes, or until they are just cooked through and the batter is golden brown and crisp. Remove the fish with a slotted spoon or slotted spatula and drain them on paper towels.

Yield: 4 to 6 servings

Fish in Herb Butter

———— ❧ ————

Any flat fish can be used instead of plaice in this recipe. I use mainly plaice because it is caught in abundance in Ballycotton Bay; the flavor is delicious when the fish is freshly caught from a small boat with a small trawl. It is much more disappointing when taken from a big trawler, as it gets bruised in the big catch. Extremely simple cooking is appropriate to fully appreciate the flavor.

1   whole plaice or small flounder
1   to 2 tablespoons unsalted butter
1½   teaspoons finely chopped mixed fresh herbs
      such as parsley, chives, fennel, and thyme
Lemon wedges

Clean the whole fish thoroughly, then lay it flat on a cutting surface. Using a very sharp knife, cut through the skin all around the fish about ½ inch from the edge. (Be sure that the cuts around the tail meet.) Lay the whole fish in a jelly-roll pan or ovenproof skillet, add about ¼ inch of water, and sprinkle the fish with salt and pepper to taste. Bake the fish in a preheated 400° F. oven for 15 to 20 minutes, or until it is cooked through.

Meanwhile in a small saucepan melt the butter and stir in the herbs. When the fish is done, gently peel the cut skin away from the whole fish, arrange the fish on a plate, and spoon the herb butter over it. Garnish with the lemon wedges.

Yield: 1 serving

POULTRY

Chicken Pie

———— ❧ ————

The best kind of old hen is one that has lain for one season in a deep-litter house: She is often very fat and full of flavor. Cook the hen in a heavy iron saucepan or kettle with a tight-fitting lid in two inches of water with some herbs and root vegetables. Various flavors—wine, leeks, tarragon, or spices—can be introduced at this stage.

The quickest way to degrease cooking juices is to use a creamer. These are big flat bowls in which milk was left standing in dairies long ago (they now have to be made specially to order). After twenty-four hours all the cream had risen to the top. "Skimmed milk" was then poured off from the bottom of the pan through a lip fitted with a guard that held back the cream. This procedure works much more quickly for a fatty stock; the fat rises in about 2 minutes.

1   5-pound stewing hen
1   onion, sliced
1   carrot, sliced
A bouquet garni, *made by tying together 1 sprig each of parsley and thyme, and 1 bay leaf*
12   *large button mushrooms (about ½ pound), quartered*
16   *peeled and blanched pearl onions or 6 scallions*
¾   *stick (6 tablespoons) unsalted butter*
5   *tablespoons all-purpose flour*
⅔   *cup dry white wine*
1   *cup heavy cream*
½   *pound lean salt pork, cut into ½-inch cubes, parboiled for 10 minutes, and drained*
10   *ounces commercial or homemade puff pastry, thawed if frozen*
An egg wash made from 1 large egg beaten with
    ¼ teaspoon salt

In a heavy kettle combine the chicken with 2 inches water, the onion, carrot, and *bouquet garni*. Bring the water to a simmer on top of the stove and bake the chicken mixture, covered, in a preheated 350° F. oven for 1 to 2 hours, or until the chicken is tender (the time will vary according to the age of the chicken). Remove the chicken from the kettle and let it cool. Remove the meat from the bones and cut it into neat slices. Strain and degrease the cooking liquid (see above) and reserve 2½ cups for the sauce.

In a large skillet cook the mushrooms and onions in the butter over moderately low heat for about 4 minutes, or until the onions are just softened. Stir in the flour and cook over medium heat, stirring, for about 2 minutes. Stir in the reserved stock, wine, and cream and bring to a boil, stirring. Off the heat stir in the pork and chicken. Taste and season with salt and pepper.

Spoon the entire mixture into a 3-quart shallow baking dish.

Roll the puff pastry on a lightly floured surface to fit the baking dish with a 1-inch overhang on all sides. Drape the pastry over the filling, crimp the edges decoratively, and brush the pastry with the egg wash. Cut 2 or 3 steam vents in the pastry and bake the pie in a preheated 450° F. oven for 15 to 20 minutes, or until the filling is hot and bubbling and the pastry is a rich golden brown. Serve hot.

Yield: 8 servings

Old-Fashioned Roast Stuffed Chicken

There are three kinds of chicken on my horizon: free-range roasting chickens; intensively reared, frozen, broiler chickens; and old hens. They all have their uses as far as I'm concerned.

The finest bird is, of course, the free-range roaster. They are not easy to come by. It is everybody's treasure hunt to find a source of supply. Go to the best poultry supplier you can find, explain what you want, and if you can, place a regular order. As a last resort perhaps you can rear your own if you don't live in a large city.

This bird makes the kind of old-fashioned Sunday dinner that your grandmother might have served at the beginning of the century. Prepare all the trimmings—a buttery fresh-herb stuffing, creamy bread sauce or Cumberland sauce, crisp rolled bacon. I always serve homemade sausages and black puddings and colcannon as well. Don't attempt this with a broiler; all your work will be wasted on the tasteless flesh.

FOR THE STUFFING
½ stick (¼ cup) unsalted butter
1 cup chopped onion
2 cups soft fresh bread crumbs
¼ cup mixed chopped fresh herbs such as parsley, thyme, chives, marjoram, savory, chervil, and/or tarragon

1 whole roasting chicken (3½ to 5 pounds), preferably free-range
2 teaspoons unsalted butter, softened
1 tablespoon rendered chicken fat (available from a butcher or at a supermarket)
1 small carrot, sliced
1 small onion, sliced
A small bouquet garni, made by tying together 1 sprig each of parsley and thyme, and 1 bay leaf

To make the stuffing, heat the butter in a skillet over moderately low heat and in it cook the onion for about 5 minutes, or until it is softened. Off the heat stir in the bread crumbs, herbs, and salt and pepper to taste.

Wash and dry the chicken, cut off the wing tips, and reserve them with the neck and the giblets (except liver) for making the gravy. Season the chicken cavity with salt and pepper. Spoon the stuffing into the cavity and truss the chicken. Rub the butter over the breast portion of the chicken and sprinkle the skin with salt and pepper.

Put the chicken on a rack in a roasting pan with the chicken fat in the bottom of the pan. Roast the chicken in a preheated 400° F. oven for 20 minutes, lower the oven temperature to 350° F., and roast the chicken, basting it occasionally with the drippings, for 45 to 60 minutes more, or until the juices run clear when a thigh is pierced with the tip of a sharp knife.

While the chicken is roasting, simmer the reserved giblets, neck, and wing tips with the carrot, onion, and *bouquet garni* in 3 cups water (or more to cover) for about 45 minutes. Strain and reserve the stock.

Transfer the chicken to a heated platter. Spoon the excess fat from the roasting pan, discarding it. Add 2 cups of the reserved stock to the pan, bring the liquid to a boil, stirring to scrape up the browned bits, and cook it over moderate heat for a few minutes, or until the gravy is thickened slightly. Season to taste with salt and pepper.

Remove the stuffing from the chicken, carve the bird, and serve it with the stuffing and gravy.

Yield: 4 to 6 servings

Baked Chicken with Creamy Leek Sauce

Broiler chickens can be deep-fried or sautéed with good results. They are also delicious when baked in a casserole with herbs, vegetables, or spices.

2   teaspoons vegetable oil
2   tablespoons plus 2 teaspoons unsalted butter
1   2½-pound whole chicken (preferably a broiler)
1½   cups sliced white part of leeks, washed well
1   tablespoon all-purpose flour
½   to 1 cup chicken stock or canned chicken broth
1   extra-large egg yolk
1   cup light cream or half-and-half

Heat the oil and 2 teaspoons of the butter in a heavy flameproof casserole large enough to hold the chicken comfortably. Sprinkle the chicken inside and out with salt and pepper to taste. Sauté the chicken, breast side down, on one side over high heat for about 5 minutes, or until that side is golden, then turn and sauté the other breast side until it too is golden. Remove the chicken from the casserole and wipe out the casserole.

Add the remaining 2 tablespoons butter to the casserole and cook the leeks in the butter over moderately low heat for 2 to 3 minutes, or until they begin to soften. Return the chicken to the casserole and bake it, covered, in a preheated 375° F. oven for 40 minutes to 1 hour, or until it is cooked through and the juices run clear when a thigh is pierced with the tip of a sharp knife.

Transfer the chicken to a heated platter and spoon the excess fat from the casserole. Add the flour and cook the mixture, stirring, over moderately low heat for 2 minutes. Add ½ cup of the stock and bring the mixture to a boil, stirring. In a small bowl whisk the egg yolk into the cream and then whisk the mixture into the stock mixture. Cook over low heat for about 2 minutes, or until thickened (do not allow to boil). If the sauce seems too thick, add as much of the remaining ½ cup stock as desired. Taste and season the sauce with salt and pepper.

Carve the chicken and coat it with the sauce.

Yield: 4 servings

Turkey White—Turkey Brown

———— ❧ ————

This is a lovely buffet recipe for a large crowd. It takes time to make in large quantities but can be prepared in advance, and the result looks very pretty on the dish. The white meat is sautéed in butter and served in a sauce of cream and lemon juice. The dark meat is served in a red-wine sauce with herbs, onions, bacon, and mushrooms.

1	15-pound whole turkey

FOR THE STOCK
1	carrot, quartered
1	onion, quartered

A bouquet garni, *made by tying together 1 large sprig each of parsley and thyme, and 1 bay leaf*

FOR EACH 1 POUND WHITE MEAT
½	cup all-purpose flour, seasoned with ¼ teaspoon salt and ⅛ teaspoon black pepper
3	tablespoons unsalted butter
2	cups heavy cream
4	teaspoons fresh lemon juice

FOR EACH 1 POUND DARK MEAT
½	cup all-purpose flour, seasoned with ¼ teaspoon salt and ⅛ teaspoon black pepper
3	tablespoons unsalted butter

1½	cups (¼ pound) sliced mushrooms
½	cup (2 ounces) chopped lean bacon
½	cup chopped onion
1	cup dry red wine
1	cup turkey stock (from above)
1	tablespoon chopped fresh herbs such as parsley or a mix of parsley and thyme

Using a sharp knife, cut the breast from the turkey in 2 large pieces, lay each half, cut side down, on a board, and slice across the grain into ¼-inch-thick scallops. Pick the meat from the wings and slice or pound it into ¼-inch-thick pieces. Do the same with all the dark meat, trying to keep the pieces as intact as possible. Reserve the meat. Cut up the turkey carcass and in a kettle combine it with the neck, giblets, and enough cold water to cover the bones. Add the

Preceding pages: The herb garden at the cooking school. At center a gray cushion of sage nestles behind a tall dill plant in full flower with overgrown tarragon in front. A bed of nasturtiums, right, is surrounded by chives in flower.

carrot and onion along with the *bouquet garni* and simmer the mixture, skimming as necessary, for 1 to 2 hours, or until the stock is intensely flavorful.

To prepare the white meat, coat the scallops with the seasoned flour, shaking off the excess. In a large skillet heat 1½ tablespoons of the butter over moderately high heat, in it sauté half the turkey scallops for 2 to 3 minutes on each side, or until golden brown and cooked through, and transfer them to a heated platter. Repeat the procedure with the remaining 1½ tablespoons butter and the remaining white meat of turkey. Add 1 cup of the cream to the skillet and bring it to a simmer, stirring to scrape up the browned bits. Pour in the remaining 1 cup cream and the lemon juice and simmer the sauce, stirring, for about 5 minutes, or until thickened slightly and reduced by about one third. Taste and season with salt and pepper. Return the turkey and any accumulated pan juices to the sauce and simmer for a few seconds, or until heated through. The mixture may be made 1 day in advance and kept covered and chilled.

To prepare the dark meat, coat the turkey with the seasoned flour, shaking off the excess, and reserve it as well as any extra seasoned flour. In a large skillet heat 1 tablespoon of the butter over moderately high heat and in it sauté the mushrooms for 1 minute. Transfer the mushrooms to a plate with a slotted spoon and reserve them. Add 1 more tablespoon butter and half the reserved turkey to the skillet, sauté the turkey scallops for 2 to 3 minutes on each side, or until golden brown and cooked through, and transfer them to a heated platter. Repeat the procedure with the remaining 1 tablespoon butter and the remaining dark meat of turkey. Add the bacon and onion to the skillet and cook, stirring, for about 5 minutes, or until the bacon is browned and the onions are softened. Stir in 2 teaspoons of the reserved seasoned flour and cook, stirring, for 1 minute. Add the wine and bring to a simmer, stirring to scrape up the browned bits. Add 1 cup of the turkey stock made above and simmer for 3 minutes. Return the mushrooms to the skillet and simmer for 3 minutes. Return the turkey and any accumulated pan juices to the sauce and simmer for a few seconds, or until heated through. The mixture may be made 1 day in advance and kept covered and chilled.

Serve the white and dark meat warm in their sauces.

Yield: 30 servings (using the entire whole turkey)

Roast Duck

I find it hard to get good results from commercially raised, frozen ducks. I was once overheard screaming down the telephone to an uncooperative co-operative manager, "Do you freeze the ducks before you kill them, then?" Back to the farmer's wife for ducks, or to an understanding poultry supplier.

This traditional method of cooking the genuine article is hard to beat.

FOR THE STUFFING
3   tablespoons unsalted butter
¾   cup chopped onion
1   tablespoon chopped fresh sage leaves
1½   cups soft fresh bread crumbs

1   5-pound duck
1   small carrot, sliced
1   small onion, sliced
A bouquet garni, *made by tying together 1 sprig each of parsley and thyme, and 1 bay leaf*

To make the stuffing, heat the butter in a skillet over moderately low heat and in it cook the onion for about 5 minutes, or until it is softened. Off the heat stir in the sage, bread crumbs, and salt and pepper to taste.

Wash and dry the duck, cutting off the wing tips and reserving them with the neck and giblets (except liver) for making the gravy. Season the duck cavity with salt and pepper. Spoon the stuffing into the cavity.

Put the duck, breast side up, on a rack in a roasting pan and roast it in a preheated 400° F.

oven for 1 hour, then lower the oven temperature to 350° F., and roast the duck, basting it occasionally with the drippings, for 30 minutes to 1 hour more, or until the juices run clear when a thigh is pierced with the tip of a sharp knife.

While the duck is roasting, simmer the reserved giblets, neck, and wing tips with the carrot, onion, and *bouquet garni* in 3 cups water (or more to cover) for about 45 minutes. Strain and reserve the stock.

Transfer the duck to a heated platter and spoon the excess fat from the roasting pan. Add 2 cups of the reserved stock to the pan, bring the liquid to a boil, stirring to scrape up the browned bits, and cook it over moderate heat for a few minutes, or until the gravy is thickened slightly. Season to taste with salt and pepper.

Remove the stuffing from the duck, carve the bird, and serve it with the stuffing and gravy.

Yield: 4 to 6 servings

Ballymaloe farmyard from the old castle gateway.

MEAT

Spiced Beef

This is an old-fashioned recipe. Nowadays saltpeter, or sodium nitrate, is regarded as a health hazard, so perhaps you should not live exclusively on this dish; certainly people have lived well for generations on occasional meals of meats preserved in this way. Saltpeter is one reason bacon once kept well, though it does no longer. Because the recipe works perfectly well without the saltpeter, it is, in this version, an optional ingredient.

4½ teaspoons Demerara (raw) sugar
1 tablespoon salt
1 tablespoon ground juniper berries
1½ teaspoons coarsely ground black pepper
1½ teaspoons ground allspice
A pinch of saltpeter (optional)
2½ to 3 pounds beef brisket or flank steak

In a small dish stir together the sugar, salt, juniper berries, pepper, allspice, and optional saltpeter. Rub the mixture into all sides of the brisket. Chill the meat in a shallow dish, covered, for at least 24 hours or up to 36 hours.

Remove the excess spice mixture, roll up the meat, and tie it with string.

When ready to cook the meat, put it in a kettle or heavy skillet and barely cover with water. Bring the water to a simmer, uncovered, and simmer the beef gently, covered tightly, for 2 to 3 hours, or until it is tender.

Serve hot or cold, sliced across the grain. If serving the spiced beef cold, weight it with a few cans or bricks on a plate or a board to press it and chill the meat for 12 hours before slicing.

Yield: about 6 servings

A roll of Spiced Beef with Tomato, Potato, and Cucumber Salads.

Tournedos with Mushrooms

———— ❧ ————

I admire tremendously the smooth organization of daily life that operated before the motor car and telephone came and enabled us to sail along thoughtlessly until the last minute. There was no rushing out at twelve-thirty to buy something for lunch in those days.

Life was pre-arranged. If visitors were coming, they had written a week before. My predecessors then sat down and wrote a postcard to the butcher at Cloyne, knowing that he would unfailingly deliver on Friday for the weekend. In summer he would deliver on Tuesdays as well. The meat was fresh; it would not have kept if it had been hung as we now require it to be. Delicious bread came every day, fresh from the village bakery in Cloyne or Castlemartyr. Eggs, vegetables, and butter were sent twice weekly to Ballycotton from Ballymaloe Farm in a little donkey cart. The boy who delivered them still works on the farm. Nowadays it is a real treasure hunt to get fresh farm eggs and vegetables in Ballycotton. Milk was delivered to Cloyne every day—twice daily in the summer—straight after milking. I don't believe that the milk that now rattles round the roads in a lorry all day is a healthier product.

Now only the Cuddigans, the butchers in Cloyne, are still in business.

The Cuddigans traditionally produced high-quality meat for the gentry of the district. The gentry have gone; their houses are now occupied mostly by families of a different stock. Young Mr. Cuddigan, however, continues to run the business the same way. He buys prime heifers and finishes fattening them on the damp lush grass in the flat fields on the south side of Cloyne. His lambs are bought with his meticulous flair for perfection; they must never have suffered a setback in growth from the day they were born. He scorns the cult for lean meat. Once this is understood, there is no problem: One is under no obligation to eat the fat. I would far prefer to fry in mutton fat than cooking oil anyway.

Tournedos are 1-inch-thick slices of beef fillet, trimmed and tied into neat rounds with string. (A butcher can do this for you.) Since the sauce is quite reduced and intense, use homemade beef stock instead of the salty canned broth available in stores.

6   slices of lean bacon, diced
¼   cup minced shallots or ½ cup chopped
     scallions
1   cup dry red wine
1   cup beef stock, preferably homemade
½   stick (¼ cup) unsalted butter
6   slices of good white bread, cut into rounds to
     fit the tournedos
2   cups sliced mushrooms
6   ¼-pound tournedos steaks
2   tablespoons vegetable oil
1   tablespoon Chicken Liver Pâté (page 34)

In a large skillet fry the bacon until it is crisp, transfer it with a slotted spoon to paper towels to drain, and pour off all but 1 tablespoon drippings. Add the shallots and sauté for 1 minute, or until they are softened. Add the wine and stock and boil the sauce to reduce it by about half.

In another large skillet heat 1 tablespoon of the butter over moderate heat and in it cook the bread, turning it, until it is golden on both sides. Remove the croutons from the skillet and reserve them. Add 1 tablespoon of the remaining butter

to the skillet and in it cook the mushrooms for about 3 minutes, or until they are softened. Remove the mushrooms from the skillet with a slotted spoon and reserve them.

Season the tournedos with pepper and sauté them over moderately high heat in the skillet in the remaining 2 tablespoons butter and the oil for about 2 minutes on each side for medium-rare meat, or until cooked to the desired degree of doneness. (This may need to be done in 2 skillets or in batches if the tournedos do not fit comfortably in a single skillet; do not crowd the meat.) Transfer the tournedos to a heated platter.

Pour the sauce into the skillet in which the meat was cooked, bring it to a boil, and boil it, stirring, until it is reduced slightly. Stir in the mushrooms and the bacon, and just before serving swirl in the pâté. Taste and correct the seasonings.

Set each tournedos atop a crouton and spoon a little sauce over the top.

Yield: 6 servings

Sauté of Calf's Liver with Whiskey Tarragon Sauce

———— ❧ ————

Unsalted, preferably homemade, beef stock is important to use here, because the reduction of the sauce concentrates the seasoning.

2   cups beef stock, preferably homemade
¼   cup all-purpose flour
⅛   teaspoon salt
⅛   teaspoon black pepper
4   ¼-pound calf's liver slices
3   tablespoons unsalted butter
¼   cup Irish whiskey
1   garlic clove, minced
1½ tablespoons minced fresh tarragon
¼   cup heavy cream

Bring the stock to a boil in a small saucepan and boil it over high heat until it is reduced to 1 cup.

Combine the flour, salt, and pepper in a shallow dish and dip the liver in the seasoned flour, coating it well. Heat the butter over moderately high heat in a large skillet and in it sauté the liver for about 2 minutes on each side for medium-rare, or until cooked to the desired degree of doneness. Transfer the meat to a heated platter.

Add the whiskey to the skillet and heat it. Ignite the whiskey carefully with a match, tipping the skillet away from you, and when the flames subside add the reduced stock, garlic, and tarragon. Boil the mixture for 1 minute, or until reduced slightly, and stir in the cream. Spoon the sauce over the liver.

Yield: 4 servings

Flowers running wild in a corner of the walled garden.

Steak and Oyster Pie

———— ❧ ————

Cheaper cuts of beef are ideal in pies such as steak and kidney, steak and oyster, or steak and pigeon. I think it is time that people went back to the meat pie. Suet crust is cheap and easy to make, but perhaps it takes a lot of exercise in the cold, fresh air to develop the right sort of metabolism to cope with it.

The oysters give a delicious flavor to the meat but dissolve somewhat in the cooking. We use individual china pie dishes for restaurant service. One night a customer complained that he could not find an oyster in his pie. After that, for a while, we put oysters in the pie dishes last thing before we put the crust on. This practice ensured that everyone could find the oysters, but the pie did not have such a good flavor.

3	tablespoons unsalted butter
1½	pounds boneless beef chuck, cut into cubes
1	large onion, chopped
1	tablespoon all-purpose flour
2½	cups beef stock or canned beef broth
12	oysters, shucked, reserving the liquor
¼	teaspoon salt
¼	teaspoon black pepper
2	cups (6 ounces) sliced mushrooms

About ¾ pound commercial or homemade puff pastry, thawed if frozen

Heat 2 tablespoons of the butter in a heavy Dutch oven and in it brown the beef over medium heat in batches (do not crowd the meat), watching carefully so that the butter does not burn and transferring it to a plate with a slotted spoon as it is done. Add the onion and cook it for 2 to 3 minutes. Stir in the flour and cook, stirring, for 2 minutes. Return the beef to the Dutch oven, add the stock, the oysters and their reserved liquor, and the salt (omit salt if using canned beef broth) and pepper and bring the mixture just to a boil. In a preheated 350° F. oven bake the mixture for about 1 hour, or until the meat is tender.

In a skillet sauté the mushrooms in the remaining 1 tablespoon butter for about 2 minutes, or until they are softened. When the meat is tender, remove the Dutch oven from the oven and stir in the mushrooms. Transfer the meat mixture to a 2-quart shallow baking dish.

Raise oven temperature to 450°F.

Roll the puff pastry out on a lightly floured surface to fit the baking dish with a 1-inch overhang on all sides. Drape the pastry over the filling, crimp the edges decoratively, and cut a steam slit in the top of the pastry with a sharp knife. Bake the pie in the center of the oven for 5 minutes, then lower the heat to 425°F. and bake the pie for 15 to 20 minutes more, or until the filling is bubbling and the pastry is golden brown and flaky. Serve immediately.

Yield: 6 servings

Lamb Noisettes in Mint Butter Sauce

— ❧ —

A late Easter with warm, damp weather upset the man who made our Easter eggs, as the chocolate was slow to set in the molds. An early Easter, however, made my butcher angry. "The churches really ought to get together and do something about it," he stormed. This was the proper purpose of ecumenism. He was never known to kill a lamb before Easter, no matter how late it was. The killing of the first lambs and Easter weekend still go together in this district.

If the lamb is ready before my mint bed, it upsets *me*. It is essential for me to have one small secret patch in a sheltered place, unknown to my friends, relations, and kitchen staff.

Very simple cooking is needed for the first lamb of the season. A chop or noisette can be sautéed quickly in butter and mint. Later on, boned and stuffed loin or shoulder is good.

Noisettes are ¾- to 1-inch-thick slices of boned loin of lamb, trimmed of surplus fat and rolled and tied into neat rounds. (A butcher can prepare the lamb for you.)

4   *slices of good white bread*
5   *tablespoons unsalted butter*
8   *2-ounce noisettes of lamb*
3   *tablespoons thinly sliced scallion*
¼   *cup dry white wine*
¼   *cup beef stock or canned beef broth*
¼   *cup chopped fresh mint plus whole mint leaves for garnish*

From each slice of bread cut 2 rounds that are the same size as the noisettes. Heat 1 tablespoon of the butter over moderate heat in a large skillet and in it cook the bread until it is golden on both sides. Remove the croutons from the skillet and reserve them.

Season the lamb with salt and pepper. In the same skillet used to cook the croutons heat 2 more tablespoons of the butter and in it sauté the lamb over moderately high heat for about 3 minutes on each side for medium-rare, or until cooked to the desired degree of doneness. (This may need to be done in batches or in 2 skillets if the noisettes do not fit comfortably in 1 skillet; do not crowd the meat.) Transfer the lamb to a heated platter.

Add the scallion to the skillet and toss over moderately low heat for 1 minute. Add the wine and stock, bring the liquid to a boil, scraping up any browned bits, and cook for 1 minute. Reduce the heat to very low and whisk in the remaining 2 tablespoons butter, cut into bits and added gradually to thicken the sauce slightly. Stir the chopped mint into the sauce, spoon the sauce over the lamb, and garnish the dish with the whole mint leaves.

Yield: 4 servings

Lamb Roast with Rosemary and Garlic

———— ❧ ————

We used to have a lovely big old rosemary bush in our garden. One cold winter it died. My daughter-in-law Hazel, who lives in the garden, accused my cooks of picking it to death. They weren't allowed in the garden again for ages. Now I know better, because a friend of mine told me that she lost three mature rosemary bushes in the ravages of that winter.

All the same, cooks are quite insensitive to gardeners' problems, and I can't agree with Constance Spry, who wrote a book called *Come into the Garden, Cook*. Gardeners also have their limitations: They have no idea how much rosemary, mint, parsley, and lettuce is needed by five cooks for ninety dinners.

You might ask, what did my cooks do with so much rosemary, even to be wrongfully accused of taking it all? Well, it would have gone mainly into legs of lamb for roasting, because this is such a nice, easy dish, one that never goes wrong. It takes time to prepare, but what a comfortable way of spending 20 minutes on a kitchen stool! You can chat as you go along, and the lamb looks so pretty when it is finished. Here is how to do it.

1   6-pound leg of lamb, bone in
2   large sprigs of rosemary plus additional
     sprigs for garnish
4   to 5 garlic cloves
2   cups beef or lamb stock (see Note)

With the point of a skewer or the tip of a sharp knife, make ½-inch-deep incisions, about 1 inch apart, all over the lamb. (We do, however, leave the underside unseasoned for serving to those who insist on plain lamb.)

Divide 2 of the rosemary sprigs into tufts of 3 or 4 needles each. Peel the garlic and cut the cloves into matchstick slivers. Insert a rosemary tuft and a garlic sliver into each incision in the lamb and chill the lamb, covered, for 24 hours.

When ready to cook, sprinkle the lamb with salt and pepper to taste and roast it in a flame-proof roasting pan in a preheated 400° F. oven for 20 minutes. Reduce the oven temperature to 350° F. and roast the lamb for approximately 1 hour more for rare meat and 1½ hours for well-done. Transfer the lamb to a heated platter and cover loosely.

Skim the fat from the roasting pan, discarding it, and add the stock to the pan juices. Bring the mixture to a boil and cook it, scraping up any browned bits, for 3 to 4 minutes, or until the sauce is reduced slightly.

Carve the lamb, garnish it with the additional rosemary sprigs, and pass the sauce separately.

Yield: 6 to 8 servings

Note: Lamb stock is wonderful here and can be made by following the directions on page 76.

Beef with Stout

From Norman times up to the 1950s, cattle were bought and sold in Ireland mainly at fairs. (Before that they had been won or lost as a result of raids, wars, and marriages. The decisive change came in 1955, when the marts were established.) A fair was held in Cloyne on the fourth Monday in every month that had five Mondays in it. A fair was held in Fermoy on the first Monday of each month, Midleton on the second, Youghal on the third, and Killeagh on the last Monday. These served the farmers of East Cork.

On the night before Cloyne fair the shopkeepers barricaded their windows with wooden planks. From three o'clock on, the next morning, farmers, their sons, and their men were up to drive their fat bullocks, stores and calves, in-calf heifers, milking cows, suckling cows with their calves, and any odds and ends of animals they had along the roads to Cloyne to be sold. Sheep and pigs were sold too, but the main business was in cattle. They stood in groups in the street and on the pavements. The town was packed, the pubs full, and what a mess was in the streets when they left in midafternoon and the shopkeepers ruefully unboarded their glass windows.

The bargaining was an expert job. My husband went in to see how things were going at about 7:30 A.M. He went to Charley Creed's house for a sumptuous gentlemen's breakfast, but he *never* attempted to make a deal. Women never went to the fair at all.

Buying and selling were done for us by Jack Smyth, who was noted for his ability to make a good deal. A lifetime of experience had taught him all the tricks of the trade. He knew all the farmers and the dealers. He arranged marriages as well, for he knew what would suit the families. Although marriages were sometimes arranged in the pubs after the fair, they usually materialized after a long period of negotiation. If Jack Smyth was involved, neither of the partners nor their families would know who was being considered for them up until a late stage in the arrangements. When Jack was going out to negotiate with a family, he drove his pony and trap in the opposite direction to the way he intended to go, so that nobody would guess who he had in mind for the match.

The marriages themselves worked surprisingly well, such was the simplicity of life and the structure and conventions of the times. But, by the 1950s, both the fairs and the arranging of marriages in this way were outdated.

Here are some quickly cooked meat dishes, all products of the cattle trade. The accompanying sauces are cheered up with a little Irish liquor, handy for supper after a fair, perhaps!

The best cuts of prime beef should be kept mainly for roasting and grilling, to be served with the classic English and French sauces. I like to offer a choice of *béarnaise*, horseradish sauce, and garlic mayonnaise with roast beef, which is served with a tomato fondue and green salad as well. A cheaper cut can be treated as a sauté and then simmered in its sauce until it is tender.

Cooking time for the stew will depend upon the quality of the beef. Rump steak would be my first choice. Cut the beef into serving portions the size and thickness of a small steak.

½   stick (¼ cup) unsalted butter
1   pound boneless beef chuck, brisket, or rump, cut into 1- by 2-inch pieces
1   large onion, sliced thin
A bouquet garni, *made by tying together 1 large sprig each of thyme, sage, and parsley, and 1 bay leaf*
¼   teaspoon salt
¼   teaspoon black pepper
1   cup beef stock or canned beef broth
¼   cup stout or dark ale
4   medium potatoes (¾ to 1 pound total), peeled
2   tablespoons chopped fresh parsley leaves

Heat half the butter over moderate heat in a kettle or large ovenproof skillet and brown the beef in batches (watch that the butter does not burn), transferring the meat to a plate with a slotted spoon as it is done. Cook the onion in the hot fat for 3 minutes, or until it is just softened. Return the meat to the kettle, add the *bouquet garni*, salt (omit if using canned broth), pepper, stock, and stout, and bring the mixture, covered, just to a boil.

Cook the stew, covered, in a preheated 350° F. oven for about 1 hour. Add the potatoes and bake the stew for 45 minutes, or until the meat and potatoes are tender. Taste and add salt and pepper if desired. Discard the *bouquet garni*. Enrich the sauce by swirling in the remaining 2 tablespoons butter. Serve the stew sprinkled with the parsley.

Yield: 3 to 4 servings

Overleaf: For farmers and fishermen, Dingle Pies provided a sustaining snack. They were the inspiration for this spiced mutton pie, which makes good picnic fare. Also shown are small crocks of Chicken Liver Pâté, Tomato Chutney, Brown Picnic Cookies, and Lemonade.

Dingle Pies (Spiced Mutton Pies)

———— ❧ ————

Pies were made for special occasions in Dingle, for Lady Day in September, Holy Thursday, and November's Day (All Saints). They were also made for fair days, when nobody had time to sit down to a proper meal but the pie shops flourished.

For the farmers and fishermen the pies provided a sustaining snack. They were made from scraps of mutton or the meat of a sheep's head, for Dingle is in mountainous sheep country. It is a sheltered meeting place before that long, wild peninsula plunges into the great Atlantic.

There were several recipes for mutton pies in and about Dingle. All are very simple. The pastry was shortened with butter, drippings, or mutton fat and sometimes moistened with hot milk. It was rolled out and cut with a saucer. The meat was seasoned and heaped in the middle, and a smaller circle of pastry, cut with a tumbler, was placed on top. The pastry base was brought up to fit over the top circle, pleated to fit, the edges moistened and pinched. The pies were baked in a slow to moderate oven for about an hour, or boiled in a stock made out of the mutton bones. Fishermen brought them to sea in a can and heated them up in the stock over a little fire made in a tin box at the bottom of the boat. A cold baked pie was better for the farmer's pocket.

The spiced mutton pies are a sophisticated descendant of Dingle Pies, inspired by them. The pastry is a rich hot-water crust made with a lot of butter. Served hot or cold, they are good for picnics.

FOR THE MUTTON OR LAMB STOCK (*optional; see Note*)

1 pound mutton or lamb bones (see below)
Peelings from 3 carrots and trimmings from any other vegetables such as onions or parsnips
Sprigs of fresh herbs such as thyme and marjoram

3 ounces mutton or lamb fat for drippings (optional) or 2 tablespoons unsalted butter, lard, or bacon fat, melted

1 pound boneless mutton or lamb shoulder
Stewing meat (have the butcher give you the bones and any excess fat trimmings, too)

1 large onion, chopped coarse
3 carrots, chopped coarse
2 tablespoons all-purpose flour
1 teaspoon cuminseed
1¼ cups mutton or lamb stock or water
¼ teaspoon salt
¼ teaspoon black pepper

FOR THE CRUST
1¾ sticks (14 tablespoons) unsalted butter
3 cups all-purpose flour
½ teaspoon salt
An egg wash, made of 1 egg yolk beaten with 1 tablespoon milk

To make the optional stock, in a kettle cover the bones, vegetable peelings and trimmings, and herbs with water by 2 inches. Bring the water to a boil, then lower the heat and simmer the mixture, partially covered, for about 2 hours. Strain and skim the fat. Reserve 1¼ cups stock for this recipe.

To make the optional drippings, chop the fat into small pieces and fry it over moderately low heat in a heavy skillet until it is rendered. Reserve 2 tablespoons drippings for this recipe.

Cut the meat into ¾-inch cubes. In a heavy 3-quart saucepan or a large skillet heat the drippings and in them cook the onion and carrot over moderately low heat for 1 to 2 minutes, or until they just begin to soften. Transfer the vegetables with a slotted spoon to a plate. Add the mutton to the pan (in batches, if necessary to avoid crowding) and sauté over moderately high heat, stirring often, until lightly browned. Add the flour and cuminseed to the browned meat, tossing to coat the meat, and cook, stirring, for 2 minutes. Return the vegetables to the pan and add the 1¼ cups reserved stock, salt (omit if using canned broth), and pepper. Bring the mixture just to a boil, then lower the heat and simmer, covered, for 1½ to 2 hours, or until the meat is tender. Taste and correct the seasonings if necessary. Let cool to lukewarm before filling the pastry.

While the meat mixture is simmering, make the crust: Combine the butter with 9 tablespoons water in a saucepan and bring to a boil. Stir the flour and salt together in a large bowl, make a well in the center, and pour the boiling butter mixture in all at once. Using a wooden spoon, stir until a soft, smooth dough that cleans the side of the bowl forms. Let the dough cool completely; it will firm up considerably. (If you are in a hurry, wrap the dough in plastic wrap and chill it for about 1 hour.)

Divide the pastry into 4 portions. Pinch off about one third of each portion and reserve these as tops for the pies. Roll out separately the remaining two thirds of each portion to about a ⅛-inch thickness. Fit the pastry into 4 ovenproof 10- to 12-ounce ramekins or pot pie dishes, leaving a ½-inch overhang. Divide the meat mixture among the pastry-lined dishes. Roll out the remaining pastry to fit the tops of the dishes, moisten the edges of the bottom crusts, and cover with the top crusts. Seal the edges by pinching them together or making a decorative edge with the tines of a fork. Using a small sharp knife, cut a steam slit in each pie. Brush with the egg wash.

Bake the pies in the lower third of a preheated 425° F. oven for 10 minutes. Reduce the heat to 375° F. and bake the pies for 20 to 25 minutes more, or until the fillings are bubbling and the crusts are golden brown.

Serve immediately or let cool and serve at room temperature. To serve, gently invert the pies onto plates and serve freestanding.

Yield: 4 servings

Note: Canned beef broth may be substituted for the lamb stock, in which case the ¼ teaspoon salt should be omitted.

Ballymaloe Irish Stew

———— ❧ ————

I spent one period of my life going around asking everyone I met, "Do you put carrots in your Irish stew?" The answer was invariably, "Yes."

My mother always put carrots in her stew; everyone in Shanagarry did too. I found carrots going into Irish stew as far north as Tipperary. The classic version has no carrots, but it is common practice to include them, in the south at any rate. As this is a traditional folk dish, I feel that common practice carries its own authority.

Originally we made Irish stew by putting alternate layers of onions, carrots, potatoes, and meat in a pot. It was seasoned, covered with water, and stewed gently for 2 hours. Very simple and enjoyable.

Later on, when my children were small, a good woman called Madge Dolan came to cook for us and brought us a new and better version, which is the basis of our present recipe.

FOR THE MUTTON OR LAMB STOCK *(optional; see Note)*
2 *pounds mutton or lamb bones*
Peelings from carrots and trimmings from any other vegetables such as onions or parsnips
Sprigs of fresh herbs such as thyme and marjoram
4 *ounces mutton or lamb fat for drippings (optional) or 3 tablespoons unsalted butter, lard, or bacon fat, melted*

3 *pounds mutton neck chops or shoulder lamb chops, bone in*
4 *carrots (about ½ pound total), quartered*
4 *onions (about ¾ pound total), quartered*
½ *teaspoon salt*
¼ *teaspoon black pepper*
4 *to 6 small potatoes (about 1 pound total)*
1 *tablespoon unsalted butter*
1 *tablespoon chopped fresh parsley leaves*
1 *tablespoon snipped fresh chives*

To make the optional stock, in a kettle cover the bones, vegetable peelings and trimmings, and herbs with cold water by 2 inches. Bring the water to a boil, then lower the heat and simmer the mixture, partially covered, for about 2 hours. Strain and skim the fat. Reserve 2½ cups stock for this recipe.

To make the optional drippings, chop the fat into small pieces and fry it over moderately low heat in a heavy skillet until it is rendered. Reserve 3 tablespoons drippings for this recipe.

Heat the 3 tablespoons reserved drippings in a heavy kettle and in it brown the chops in batches (do not crowd the meat). Return the meat to the kettle and add the carrots, onions, salt (omit if using canned broth), pepper, and the 2½ cups reserved stock. Peel the potatoes and put them on top. Simmer the stew gently, covered, for 1½ to 2 hours, or until the meat is

tender. Transfer the meat and vegetables to individual bowls with a slotted spoon. Skim the fat from the stock, then taste and correct seasonings as necessary. Swirl in the butter, parsley, and chives and ladle the sauce over the meat and vegetables.

Yield: about 4 servings

Note: Canned beef broth may be substituted for the lamb stock, in which case the ½ teaspoon salt should be omitted.

VEGETABLES

Potato Salad

Potatoes are best when tossed in their dressing while they are still hot. They can then be kept for a day or two without losing flavor.

2½ pounds potatoes (unpeeled), quartered
½ cup Billy's French Dressing (page 24) or other vinaigrette
2 tablespoons chopped fresh parsley leaves
2 tablespoons snipped fresh chives or chopped scallions or onion
½ cup mayonnaise

Cook the potatoes in a saucepan of boiling salted water for 15 to 20 minutes, or until tender but not falling apart. Drain well. As soon as the potatoes can be comfortably handled, peel and cut them into ½-inch dice. Toss the warm potatoes in a bowl with Billy's French Dressing, the parsley, and chives. Let the salad cool slightly, then toss with the mayonnaise and season with salt and pepper. Let the potato salad stand at least 1 hour before serving to allow the dressing to be absorbed.

Yield: 6 servings

Potato Salad Border

Mashed potato salad is very useful for piping around platters of cold meats, fish, and vegetable salads. Use a 1-inch star tip for large dishes and a ½-inch, rather open tip for bordering scallop shells. The shells can be filled with a variety of different things such as shellfish, smoked ham, salmon, eggs, tomatoes, scallions, watercress, lettuce, etc.

2 cups mashed potatoes, warm or at room temperature
2 to 3 tablespoons Billy's French Dressing (page 24) or other vinaigrette
2 to 3 tablespoons mayonnaise
2 tablespoons minced fresh parsley leaves
2 tablespoons snipped fresh chives

In a bowl blend all ingredients together until smooth, using enough French Dressing and mayonnaise to make a firm piping consistency. Spoon the mixture into a pastry bag and pipe decorative borders around meat or salad platters.

Yield: about 2½ cups

Champ (or Stelk)

— ❧ —

I like to pick fresh onions as they grow in the fields and garden before their green stalks wither. This kind of onion cooked with part of the green top gives a new dimension to every dish in which it is used. It is best of all in Champ.

2   pounds potatoes, scrubbed
1   cup chopped scallions or ½ cup snipped fresh chives
1   to 1½ cups milk
½   to 1 stick (¼ to ½ cup) unsalted butter

In a large saucepan cook the potatoes in boiling salted water for 30 to 40 minutes, or until tender. While the potatoes are cooking, simmer the scallions, if using, in a saucepan in 1 cup of the milk for 5 minutes, or until they are soft, and strain them, reserving the milk as well as the scallions. Drain the potatoes well, then peel and mash them with 1 cup of the milk (use the strained milk here, if using the scallions), adding the remaining ½ cup if necessary to make a soft consistency. Stir in the chives, if using, and season with salt and pepper.

Spoon the champ into a serving dish, make a hollow in the center, and put the butter in the hollow to melt slowly into the mixture.

Yield: 6 servings

Buttered Onions with Thyme

— ❧ —

B uttered Onions make a delicious vegetable to serve with roasted or grilled meat or poultry. They are sturdy enough to be kept warm for some time before service, whereas a green vegetable would be ruined. They can also be added to a meat sauce for extra flavor.

1½   tablespoons unsalted butter
½   pound pearl onions, blanched, peeled, and trimmed, leaving the root end intact, or large scallions, trimmed to within 1 inch of the root
1½   teaspoons chopped fresh thyme

Melt the butter in a heavy saucepan over low heat and toss the onions in the butter. Add 1 tablespoon water and the thyme, lay a piece of buttered waxed paper or the wrapper from a stick of butter over the onions, and cook the onions, covered tightly, over very low heat for 15 to 25 minutes, or until they are soft but not mushy.

Transfer the onions to a serving dish with a slotted spoon. If there is a lot of liquid left in the pan, boil it down to a glaze and then spoon it over the onions.

Yield: 3 to 4 servings

Colcannon

I found it really impossible to keep a house the size of mine and look after six children single-handedly. Fortunately, somebody always turned up to help. One year it was Eileen. She was cheerful, quick, and intelligent; I became dependent on her. One week she asked for her half day on a Wednesday instead of a Thursday, and I didn't see her again for some while. Neither did her mother. We didn't know where she was, but on Wednesdays the boat sailed for England and someone had seen her on the quays. A month later she turned up as unexpectedly as she had left and tearfully came to see me. "Well, if you went to London," I said, "why did you come back again?" "I couldn't eat the potatoes," she sobbed.

British Queen are the potatoes we like to eat in summer, and Kerr's Pink followed by Golden Wonder in winter. They are very floury and inclined to break in the cooking water. They should never be peeled before cooking. If they still break, the water must be poured off before they are quite cooked so that the potatoes finish cooking in their own steam. They are peeled at table and (ideally) eaten with a big lump of golden butter.

A great many Irish potato dishes exist, and there is some confusion about their names. The two we usually serve are colcannon, which is made with cabbage, and champ, or stelk, made with chives or scallions.

---

2   *pounds potatoes, scrubbed*
1   *small head of cabbage (about 1 pound), cored and shredded*
1   *to 1½ cups milk*
½   *to 1 stick (¼ to ½ cup) unsalted butter*

In a large saucepan cook the potatoes in boiling salted water for 30 to 40 minutes, or until tender. While the potatoes are cooking, cook the cabbage in a saucepan in a small amount of boiling water for 5 to 7 minutes, or until tender, and drain very well. Drain the potatoes well, then peel and mash them with enough of the milk to make a soft consistency. Stir the cabbage into the potatoes, then season with salt and pepper.

Spoon the colcannon into a serving dish, make a hollow in the center, and put the butter in the hollow to melt slowly into the mixture.

Yield: 6 servings

Mushrooms à la Crème

---❧---

My husband, Ivan, first started to grow mushrooms in 1937. He was already growing apples in the fields, and tomatoes and cucumbers in greenhouses. We were coming toward the end of the period when, in addition to the world Depression, Ireland was locked into the "Economic War" with England, and ordinary farming was in a disastrous state, as we could not sell our produce. At the same time the government, led by Eamon de Valera, was encouraging Irish industry, including the infant greenhouse industry, and mushroom growing was smiled on also.

Wild mushrooms are available in Ireland for only a few weeks every two or three years. At that, they are only for those who know where to find them. With a continuous supply of cultivated mushrooms, my husband took gifts of them to friends and relations when he visited.

In 1942 I had finished school and decided to leave home, intending to return a year later to settle down to marriage. First, I went to Northern Ireland to work in a hostel for old people who had been bombed out or otherwise dislodged from their homes by war. It was my job to clean the hostel, collect the milk from the nearest farm, prepare the vegetables, and wash up. When Ivan came to visit me he brought me a present of button mushrooms. Jubilantly I started to cook them for staff supper. I threw them on the pan but could not get them to soften; they were like bullets. Later I discovered that only flat mushrooms cook easily in a skillet; button ones need to be sliced or quartered as in the following recipe.

½	stick (¼ cup) unsalted butter
1¼	cups finely chopped onion
5	cups sliced mushrooms
2	tablespoons chopped fresh parsley leaves
1	tablespoon snipped fresh chives (optional)
⅔	cup heavy cream
2	teaspoons fresh lemon juice

Heat 2 tablespoons of the butter in a large skillet over moderately low heat and in it cook the onions for 5 minutes, or until softened. Transfer the onions to a plate with a slotted spoon.

Add 1 tablespoon of the remaining butter to the skillet, add half the mushrooms, and cook them, stirring occasionally, for 3 to 5 minutes, or until softened. Transfer the cooked mushrooms to the plate of onions, add the remaining mushrooms with the remaining 1 tablespoon butter to the skillet, and cook them until softened.

Return the mushrooms and onions on the plate to the skillet, stir in the parsley, optional chives, and cream, and bring the mixture to a simmer. Stir in the lemon juice. Taste and season with salt and pepper.

Yield: 4 to 6 servings

Onions Monégasque

———— ❧ ————

We make Onions Monégasque every week, and I have a job to find the small onions that I need for it. I don't live near the sort of market where I can just order what I want and it comes. In spring I have to wait until the first onions of the new crop are big enough to pick. I cheat and leave a lot of the stem on as well so as to make up the weight. When we have onions growing in the fields, I search around the edges for little ones that have not grown very well. Once the crops are being graded, I can get bags of them out of the machines, but they will not last until the next spring. Quite often I have to resort to cutting big ones into thick, wide rings instead.

1	*pound pearl onions, blanched, peeled, and trimmed, or large scallions, trimmed*
1	*cup tomato purée*
½	*cup white-wine vinegar*
1	*tablespoon olive oil*
3	*tablespoons sugar*
1	*teaspoon chopped fresh thyme*
½	*bay leaf*
1	*sprig of parsley*
½	*cup seedless raisins*

Combine the onions, tomato purée, vinegar, oil, sugar, thyme, bay leaf, parsley, and 1½ cups water in a non-reactive saucepan and bring the mixture to a boil. Stir in the raisins, lower the heat to a bare simmer, and simmer for about 30 minutes, or until the onions are tender. Taste and season with salt and pepper. Let the mixture cool completely. The mixture may be made 3 days in advance and kept covered and chilled.

Yield: about 6 servings

Preceding pages: Sweet peas in the walled garden.

Red Cabbage and Apples

My neighbor, Else Schiller, taught me how to cook red cabbage. She explained to me that in Germany, where she comes from, she first went to the market stall to buy a head of cabbage. Next she carried the cabbage to the place where apples were sold. She had the vendor weigh the cabbage and give her an equal weight of apples. At home, she prepared the cabbage and put it in the pot with the water and flavorings. While the mixture was heating up, she peeled the apples, set them on top, and covered the pot. She said it was important not to stir the apples in until the last moment, when the cabbage underneath had cooked.

1   1-pound head of red cabbage, cored and
    shredded
2   tablespoons cider vinegar
6   tablespoons sugar
1   teaspoon salt
1   pound McIntosh apples

Combine the cabbage, vinegar, sugar, salt, and ½ cup water in a non-reactive saucepan or skillet and bring the liquid to a boil. Peel and quarter the apples, lay them over the cabbage, and simmer the mixture gently, covered, for about 30 minutes, or until the apples and cabbage are tender. (The apples will break down into a pulp.) Check after about 20 minutes and, if there is a lot of liquid, partially uncover the pan to allow most of the liquid to evaporate. Stir the mixture together just before serving.

Yield: 4 to 6 servings

Celery for the winter; ripe sugar snap peas, and a big patch of red cabbage coming on in the garden in August.

Traditional Salad

This salad is usually served with cold meat as a luncheon or supper dish. It was and still is almost universally eaten on Sunday nights with a slice from the midday joint. The meat would have just cooled and would still be succulent from the larder—its flavor and texture do not survive in a refrigerator. This is an excellent and easy meal on the one night of the week when nobody wants to work. When I was a child, it was served in a large cut-glass bowl with a silver salad server and a sauceboat of dressing. One hunted for choice pieces of tomato and egg hiding among the lettuce leaves. Wooden bowls and servers became fashionable later on. The salad makes a good starter at dinner, served with a tiny jug of Lydia's Cream Dressing.

½	cup sugar
1	cup water
½	cup vinegar
8	slices of cooked beets
1¼	cups of Lydia's Cream Dressing (page 25)
2	cups mixed whole soft lettuce leaves such as Bibb, red-leaf, or Boston
2	large eggs, hard-boiled and quartered
2	small tomatoes, quartered
12	slices of cucumber
4	large sprigs of watercress
4	sprigs of young mustard leaves

Dissolve the sugar in the water and stir in the vinegar. Marinate the beets in this dressing for several hours.

Arrange the lettuce leaves on 4 individual plates or a serving bowl in a blossom pattern, with larger leaves on the outside and smaller leaves in the middle. Arrange the eggs, tomatoes, beets, cucumber, watercress, and mustard leaves attractively over the lettuce and between the leaves. Sprinkle the extra chopped egg whites from the dressing over the salad. Pass Lydia's Cream Dressing separately.

Yield: 4 servings

DESSERTS

Crème Brûlée

---❧---

I don't know where Mrs. Baker is now. She stayed only one night, long ago. She left this lovely recipe behind with me. She said she had cooked it for the Countess of Rosse. I think she got it from Constance Spry. It makes the nicest *crème brûlée*. The top is like smooth, shining mahogany and seals in the soft custard underneath. At first sight, people are puzzled as to how to get into it.

If the custard is not properly set, or if the skin that forms on top during cooking is broken, the caramel will sink to the bottom of the dish. If this problem arises, freeze the pudding for 1 to 2 hours before spooning on the hot caramel.

1¾ cups heavy cream
3   extra-large egg yolks
⅔   cup plus 1 tablespoon sugar

In a heavy saucepan heat 1½ cups of the cream to just below the boiling point. In a bowl whisk the egg yolks and 1 tablespoon of the sugar until thickened. Pour the hot cream in a slow stream into the yolk mixture, whisking, transfer the mixture to the pan, and cook it over low heat, stirring constantly with a wooden spoon, for 5 minutes, or until the custard coats the back of the spoon. (Do not let the custard come to a boil or it will curdle.)

Pour the custard into a shallow 1-quart dish, or one that will hold the custard to a depth of no more than 1 to 1½ inches. Chill the custard, uncovered, for at least 12 hours or overnight.

In a small heavy saucepan combine the remaining ⅔ cup sugar and ¼ cup water and cook the mixture over medium heat, stirring, until it comes to a boil and the sugar is dissolved. Continue to cook until the syrup thickens and is caramelized to a nutty brown color. Remove from the heat and carefully spoon the caramel

Rory O'Connell, the "Sorcerer's Apprentice," puts the top on a crème brûlée.

Herbs in full bloom in the walled garden.

syrup immediately over the chilled custard, covering the surface completely with a thin layer. Let the topping cool completely. Beat the remaining ¼ cup cream in a bowl until it holds soft peaks, spoon it into a pastry bag fitted with a small plain or star tip, and pipe it in a narrow line around the edge of the caramelized topping to seal the point where it meets the side of the dish.

Serve immediately or chill no more than 2 hours (if chilled longer the caramel may begin to liquefy). To serve, crack the top by tapping it sharply with the back of a serving spoon.

Yield: 4 servings

Rhubarb Compote

———— ❧ ————

I f you want people to enjoy rhubarb, use a good variety and make it sweet enough. The rhubarb we use comes from my grandfather's stock, which he planted on his farm outside Cork about one hundred years ago. It is a delicious red variety with no name we can trace.

When I was about ten, I spent a month with a favorite cousin. We used to "steal" rhubarb from his mother's garden and cook it for ourselves in her kitchen. This episode gave me a lasting love for rhubarb.

The following recipe is also suitable for many other fruits, such as red currants, black currants, gooseberries, and plums. Sometimes we flavor the syrup by boiling an elder flower or sweet geranium leaves in it before adding the fruit.

3   cups sugar
2   pounds young, slender rhubarb stalks, cut into
    1- to 1½-inch pieces
1   cup heavy cream

Combine the sugar with 3 cups water in a large non-reactive saucepan or kettle, bring the mixture to a boil, stirring constantly to dissolve the sugar, and boil it for 2 minutes. This poaching syrup may be made 2 weeks in advance and kept covered and chilled. Reheat it before using.

Add the rhubarb to the syrup and poach it gently for 6 to 10 minutes, or until it is tender but still holds its shape. Let the fruit cool, then serve at room temperature or chilled with the cream, passed separately in a pitcher, for pouring over the dessert.

Yield: about 8 servings

Gooseberry Fool

———— ❧ ————

We associate gooseberries with the first hot days in June, when wild elderberry bushes are covered in their white lacy flowers, ready for the gooseberries. Gooseberries served chilled for dessert herald the glorious long season of soft summer berries. In a period of eight weeks, one variety succeeds another in the steady march of summer. The excitement at table is constantly being renewed. If this week we have the first gooseberries, in a fortnight the first ripe strawberries come in. After a three-week gap we have raspberries, to be followed by loganberries and red, black, and white currants. The excitement at table is matched by hard work in the kitchen, with any amount of preparing, jam making, bottling, and now, mercifully, freezing the surplus fruit for winter. Oh! what a deliciously bountiful but frantic time of the year, when in Ballymaloe we are also packed with visitors on their summer holidays and the work mounts to an all but impossible level.

Gooseberry Fool is best served with soft dark-brown sugar, pouring cream, and Jane's Shortbread Cookies (page 131). As children we were allowed to crumble sweetened whole-wheat cookies over our plate of fool, making the most delicious crunchy topping for our pudding.

4 cups (about 1 pound) fresh gooseberries
1 large elder flower (optional)
1 to 1½ cups sugar
1 cup heavy cream, whipped

Combine the gooseberries with ⅓ cup water and the optional elder flower in a heavy non-reactive saucepan and simmer, stirring, for 5 to 10 minutes, or until the fruit is very soft. (Watch carefully that the fruit does not burn in the small amount of liquid.) Strain the gooseberries through a sieve into a bowl, pressing on them, or put them through a food mill. Stir 1 cup of the sugar into the hot fruit purée, taste and correct for sweetness, using the remaining ½ cup sugar if necessary and stirring until dissolved. Chill the sweetened purée until it is cooled completely and fold in the whipped cream. Spoon the fool into small stemmed glasses, dessert dishes, or a large cut-glass bowl.

Yield: about 6 servings

Overleaf: A garden at Ballycotton.

Soufflé Omelette

This soufflé omelette makes a delicious last-minute dessert. It is difficult to serve in a restaurant as it cannot be made in less than ten minutes, and with any hitch this could become a disastrous half hour. One night this happened. Paddy, my fourteen-year-old apprentice chef, and I worked as fast as we could, but reports of the party's impatience kept coming to us. Finally we got the enormous omelette (it was made in a big pan) safely onto its sugared paper. Paddy held the serving dish while I began the complicated double turn of the omelette. When it got to the stage of its somersault onto the dish he was holding, it all became too frightening: A big, hot, golden wave was heading straight for his unprotected hands. He screamed and let the dish drop, the omelette following its descent to the floor.

My son-in-law was in charge of the dining room. He surveyed the scene and went straight to his difficult customers. "I'm sorry, sir," he said to the host without flicking an eyelid, "but your omelette is in the middle of the kitchen floor!" They rocked with laughter and waited quite cheerfully for another one.

FOR THE SAUCE

1½   *cups fresh raspberries, strawberries, or blackberries*
½   *cup sugar*
2   *teaspoons Kirsch*

¼   *cup sugar*
6   *extra-large eggs, separated, reserving 2 of the yolks for another use*
2   *teaspoons unsalted butter*
½   *cup heavy cream, chilled*

To make the sauce, combine the berries and sugar in a heavy saucepan and bring slowly to a boil, stirring constantly. Boil for 1 minute, then remove the pan from the heat and stir in the Kirsch. The sauce may be made several hours in advance. Shortly before making the omelette, gently rewarm the sauce.

Put a 12-inch square of wax paper on a work surface and sprinkle it with 1 tablespoon of the sugar. In a large bowl whisk 4 of the egg yolks with the remaining 3 tablespoons sugar until the mixture is thick and pale. In another bowl beat the egg whites until they just hold stiff peaks but are not dry. Gently fold the whites into the yolk mixture until no streaks of yellow remain.

Melt the butter in a 9-inch ovenproof omelette pan. Pour the soufflé mixture into the pan and smooth the top. Cook over low heat, undisturbed, for 4 minutes, then place the pan in the middle of a preheated 375° F. oven for about 5 minutes, or until the top of the soufflé is lightly browned and puffed. While the soufflé is cooking, whip the cream in a bowl.

Gently loosen the edge of the soufflé from the pan with a small spatula, then invert the pan onto the sugared wax paper to turn out the soufflé omelette. Spread the omelette with some of the warm fruit sauce and some of the whipped cream and, using the wax paper as a guide, fold it in half. Slide the omelette to one edge of the work surface and use the paper to help you invert it onto a serving platter. Serve it immediately with the remaining berry sauce and whipped cream on the side.

Yield: 4 servings

Lemon Soufflé

This recipe is not a true soufflé at all. I don't know where it came from. The pudding arrived in our household in the late 1930s, I think, among much excitement on the part of my mother and my aunts. It's odd to make, trying to cream so little butter into so much sugar, but it works. The top is light and spongy. The bottom is a sticky lemon sauce.

1 *cup sugar*
1 *tablespoon butter, softened*
2 *extra-large eggs, separated, the whites at room temperature*
3 *tablespoons all-purpose flour*
1 *large lemon*
1 *cup milk*

Butter a 1-quart soufflé dish or other deep baking dish.

In a bowl with an electric mixer beat the sugar and butter together until the mixture is combined well and resembles coarse meal. Beat in the egg yolks, flour, and 1½ teaspoons grated rind and 2½ tablespoons juice from the lemon. Add the milk in a slow stream, beating constantly.

In another bowl beat the egg whites until they hold stiff peaks. Fold them into the lemon mixture gently but thoroughly. Pour the batter into the soufflé dish and bake in the middle of a preheated 350° F. oven for about 40 minutes, or until the top is a rich golden brown and springs back when touched with the fingertips. Let the soufflé cool slightly and serve it warm by spooning out portions of both the top "cake" layer and the bottom "sauce."

Yield: 4 to 6 servings

Caramel Mousse

A tragic story goes with the Caramel Mousse. First, you should know about the Anglo-Irish. The name was applied mainly to estate owners in the countryside. Owners of smaller farms were just called either Protestants or Catholics. The Anglo-Irish were mostly educated in England, so they spoke differently, more closely to upper-class English accents; and, although the majority were quite badly off, they had style and every now and then brought a swish of glamour to the quiet countryside of the 30s, 40s, and 50s, which livened up life for many villagers. The bitter injustices of the seventeenth, eighteenth, and nineteenth centuries were completely finished after 1922, and it should be remembered, in fairness, that the Anglo-Irish, like all people, were both good and bad and that amongst their numbers were many cultured and sports-loving people, and Irish patriots too.

In the 50s the son of our local estate owner came back to live at home with his beautiful American wife and two adorable children. We were all bowled over by the American lady's style and beauty, the cut of her clothes, her charm, and the way she decorated her house. To our great excitement we were invited to dinner with them—I suppose because we had by now scraped up enough loans and cash to buy someone else's estate.

Everything was an eye-opener for me there. To think that we had all this style from the outside world just down the road. The conversation ranged from London to New York and back to Cloyne via Rome. Well! But of all these things, I was most impressed by her Caramel Mousse. Then came tragedy. When the people of Cloyne woke up one morning, she had gone. A hemorrhage in the night could not be coped with in a remote rural area. The family moved. All that I have left of those heady days is her recipe.

1   cup sugar
4   extra-large egg yolks
1   envelope (2½ teaspoons) unflavored gelatin
¾   cup heavy cream, chilled

Combine the sugar and ½ cup water in a heavy saucepan and bring to a boil, stirring constantly, until the sugar is dissolved. Continue to boil for 10 minutes, or until the syrup caramelizes to a rich chestnut brown color. (Watch carefully as soon as the syrup begins to take on a caramel color, for it will darken quickly and could burn.) Remove the pan from the heat and, standing back from the pan to avoid splatters, slowly pour ½ cup hot water into the side of the pan. If the caramel hardens, return it to low heat and stir until it dissolves into a thick syrup.

In a bowl with an electric mixer beat the yolks to combine them, then with the mixer at medium-low speed pour the caramel syrup into the yolks in a thin stream. Increase the speed to medium-high and beat the mixture until it is completely cooled, fluffy, at least doubled in bulk, and thickened to a mousse consistency.

While the mousse is being beaten, in a small bowl soften the gelatin in 2 tablespoons cold water, then dissolve it by setting it into a larger bowl of hot water or in a microwave oven for a few seconds. In another bowl whip the cream until it holds soft peaks. Stir the dissolved gelatin into the thickened mousse until blended, then fold in the whipped cream.

Spoon into a 1½-quart serving dish and chill for 3 to 4 hours, or until firm and cold.

Yield: 6 to 8 servings

Caramel Sauce

This sauce is a good accompaniment to certain plain sweets. It will also improve a block of bought vanilla ice cream. Try it with Carrageen Moss Pudding (page 104) as well as with rice or custard puddings.

1   cup sugar

Combine the sugar with ⅓ cup hot water in a heavy saucepan and bring to a boil, stirring constantly to dissolve the sugar. Continue to boil, undisturbed, for 10 minutes, or until the syrup reaches a rich caramel color. (Watch carefully as soon as the syrup begins to color, for it will darken quickly and may burn.) Remove the pan from the heat and, standing back to avoid splattering, slowly pour 1 cup hot water into the side of the pan. If the caramel hardens, return it to low heat and stir until it is dissolved and smooth.

Yield: about 1½ cups

VARIATION

Irish Coffee Sauce

This variation on the plain Caramel Sauce above may be used in all the same combinations, but is especially good ladled over coffee ice cream.

Make the caramel as above, but substitute 1 cup hot brewed coffee for the 1 cup hot water added at the end. Let the sauce cool, then stir in 1 tablespoon Irish whiskey.

Carrageen Moss Pudding

Ballyandreen is a tiny fishing village by a rocky inlet four miles south of Ballymaloe. For generations the inhabitants there have gathered and sold carrageen moss. It is picked from the farthest-out rocks at low water during spring tides in June. This means that it is almost always covered by sea water. It is then laid out on the short grass on the clifftop to dry and bleach in the sun. The moss has the reputation of being a health-giving food. It is a source of agar jelly and certainly contains iron and minerals. Traditionally, it was fed to calves and made into cough syrups and milk puddings. I have used it all my life. I have thickened milk for babies with it at weaning time. For more sophisticated meals I serve it topped with whipped cream and coffee sauce strongly laced with whiskey.

Chocolate carrageen brings back nostalgic memories for me. I first encountered it at Sunday night supper in this house, long ago, when the place was still clad in its Victorian décor and life was very different.

The success of this dish is in using only just enough to get a set—so that you don't taste it in the pudding, as an unenthusiastic friend pointed out! A product that is hard to measure, however, is hard to market. This is so with carrageen moss. Sometimes called Irish moss, carrageen moss is available at some specialty foods shops. Carrageen sometimes comes mixed with grass and other seaweeds; these should be carefully removed before use.

½   cup (about 1 generous fistful) cleaned, well-dried carrageen moss
3¾   cups milk
1   vanilla pod or ½ teaspoon vanilla extract
3   tablespoons sugar
1   extra-large egg, separated
Fruit compote or Caramel or Irish Coffee sauces as accompaniments (optional)

Soak the carrageen in a bowl of lukewarm water for 10 minutes. Remove it from the water and combine it in a saucepan with the milk and the vanilla pod, if using. Bring the milk to a boil, then lower the heat and simmer very gently for 20 minutes. Pour the mixture through a sieve into a bowl, discarding the pod. The carrageen will now be swollen and exuding jelly. Force all this jelly through the sieve and whisk it into the milk with the sugar, egg yolk, and vanilla extract, if using.

In another bowl beat the egg white until it holds stiff peaks and fold it into the carrageen mixture. (The mixture will separate, and a fluffy top will form.) Chill the pudding for 2 to 4 hours, or until it is set, and serve it with a fruit compote or the Caramel or Irish Coffee sauces.

Yield: 4 to 6 servings

Vanilla Ice Cream

It must have been about 1950 when we got our first refrigerator. My husband teased me because I started to make ice cream while the delivery men were still carrying it into the house. Disappointment and years of failure followed as I tried out different recipes for freezing in the ice compartment. Then I bought ice-cream makers, but they all broke down, one after another. Finally I discovered the secret was to make my ice creams on an egg mousse base with whipped cream and flavoring added. Ice creams made in this way have a smooth texture and do not need further beating during the freezing period. They should not be served frozen hard.

¼ cup sugar
2 extra-large egg yolks
½ teaspoon vanilla extract
1¼ cups heavy cream, chilled

Combine the sugar with ½ cup water in a small saucepan and bring to a boil, stirring to dissolve the sugar. Cover the pan for 1 to 2 minutes, or until the sugar crystals clinging to the side are dissolved, then uncover and cook to 238°F. on a candy thermometer.

In a bowl with an electric mixer beat the egg yolks. When the syrup is ready, continue beating the yolks and slowly drizzle the hot syrup into the yolks. Continue beating on medium-high speed until the mixture is light, fluffy, and thickened to the consistency of a mousse. Beat in the vanilla. In another bowl whip the cream and fold it into the mousse. Pour the mixture into a bowl and freeze it for at least 4 hours or up to 24 hours. Remove it from the freezer compartment about 10 minutes before serving.

Yield: 6 servings (about 3½ cups)

Chocolate Ice Cream

This is essentially an elaboration of Vanilla Ice Cream. It is not too sweet, but it *is* rich.

2 ounces semisweet chocolate, chopped
1 ounce unsweetened chocolate, chopped
1 recipe Vanilla Ice Cream (page 105), prepared
   up to the point of adding the vanilla

Melt the chocolates together in the top of a double boiler set over hot water or in a low oven. Let cool slightly.

Stir the melted chocolate into the mousse along with the vanilla. Fold in the whipped cream.

Pour the mixture into a bowl and freeze it for at least 4 hours or up to 24 hours. Remove it from the freezer compartment about 10 minutes before serving.

Yield: 6 servings (about 3¾ cups)

Praline Ice Cream

Another recipe based on our Vanilla Ice Cream, this has homemade praline powder folded in.

⅔ cup unpeeled whole almonds
¼ cup sugar
1 recipe Vanilla Ice Cream (page 105),
   unfrozen

Combine the almonds and sugar in a small, heavy saucepan and cook over medium heat, stirring, for 10 minutes, or until the sugar melts, caramelizes, and coats the almonds with a dark golden syrup. Transfer to an oiled slab or baking sheet, spreading the almonds into a single layer, and let cool completely. Crush the almonds with a rolling pin or in a food processor to make a coarse powder. (You will use 3 tablespoons of the praline powder in the ice cream. The remainder keeps, stored in an airtight container, for several weeks.)

Prepare the Vanilla Ice Cream and freeze until it just begins to set. Fold in 3 tablespoons of the praline powder and continue freezing the ice cream as directed. Remove it from the freezer compartment about 10 minutes before serving.

Yield: 6 servings (about 3¾ cups)

Irish Apple Cake, Strawberry Shortcake, Chocolate Ice Cream, and Iced Chocolate Oranges on the dessert trolley.

Almond Meringue Gâteau with Chocolate and Rum Cream

I f you love to make emulsion sauces, that is, hollandaise, *béarnaise*, mayonnaise, and so on, you have a problem. It is a surplus of egg whites. Fortunately they will keep for a while in a jar in the fridge. Some can be used in batter or fruit fools, for beating into mashed potatoes, or for glazing the tops of pies. After that, meringues it must be.

Do not start to make meringues without silicone-finished paper (called parchment paper in the U.S.) to bake them on. The paper used to be hard to find. It popped up in different places at different times. I used to get it from London, Dublin, Cork, and New York—quite a shopping feat, I can tell you, when one is tied to a farm in the deep country of southeastern Cork. Fortunately, I have some friends around!

Warning: The presence of any oil, grease, or egg yolk will prevent egg whites from whipping to the correct consistency for meringues. Coffee, nuts, and orange rind all contain oil. The meringue will fail when these are added unless great care is taken to beat the whites to very dry, stiff peaks before the final addition of sugar and flavoring. The meringues should then be put into the oven as quickly as possible and baked before the oil starts to work on the mixture.

FOR THE MERINGUES
⅓ cup blanched and skinned almonds
2 extra-large egg whites at room temperature
¾ cup plus 2 tablespoons confectioners' sugar

FOR THE CHOCOLATE AND RUM CREAM
1 ounce semisweet chocolate, chopped
½ ounce unsweetened chocolate, chopped
¾ cup heavy cream, all but 1 tablespoon chilled
1 tablespoon dark rum

8 skinned whole almonds, cut in half lengthwise and toasted

To make the meringues, line a baking sheet with parchment paper and draw two 7½-inch circles on the paper, using a baking pan or template as a guide. Chop the almonds fine in a spice or nut grinder or in a food processor along with 1 tablespoon of the confectioners' sugar. In the large bowl of an electric mixer beat the egg whites with the remaining confectioners' sugar at medium-low speed until the whites just form soft peaks. Increase the speed to medium-high and beat until the mixture forms stiff peaks. Fold in the chopped almonds.

Divide the meringue between the 2 measured circles and spread evenly out to the edges. (Some people may find a pastry bag makes this step easier.) Bake in the middle of a preheated 300° F. oven for 40 to 50 minutes, or until crisp on the outside and lightly colored. Let the meringues cool slightly on the baking sheet, then carefully peel the paper from the bottoms and let the meringues cool completely on a rack. (If the meringues begin to crack as you remove the paper, don't worry. Simply stick them back together. They will be frosted and the cracks won't show.) The meringues may be made 1 day in advance and stored in an airtight container, with wax paper separating them.

To make the filling, melt the chocolates together in the top of a double boiler set over hot water or in a low oven. Blend in the 1 tablespoon unchilled cream and the rum until smooth. Let cool to room temperature. While the chocolate mixture is cooling, whip the remaining cream in a bowl. Carefully but thoroughly fold the cooled chocolate mixture into the whipped cream until blended.

Use two thirds of the filling to sandwich the meringues together, using the better-looking meringue for the top. Spoon the remaining filling into a pastry bag with a decorative tip, pipe rosettes or some other decorative border onto the top, and stud the rosettes or border with the almonds. The dessert may be assembled a few hours in advance and chilled, loosely covered.

Yield: 6 servings

Iced Chocolate Cases with Rum Cream

---- ❧ ----

The chocolate cases in this recipe are filled with chocolate ice cream. Alternatively one could fill them with any store-bought or homemade ice cream, with a pastry cream and strawberries, or with a liqueur and small fruits.

6   ounces semisweet chocolate, chopped
2   ounces unsweetened chocolate, chopped
2   to 2½ cups Chocolate Ice Cream (page 106), softened
½   cup heavy cream, chilled
1   teaspoon sugar
1   tablespoon dark rum

Have ready 16 paper cupcake liners and combine them to make 8 double-thickness liners.

Melt the chocolates together in the top of a double boiler set over hot water or in a low oven. Brush the melted chocolate in a *very* thin layer to cover the bottom and side of each double-thickness paper liner. Set the liners in a cupcake pan and chill them, or set them in the freezer for a few minutes, to harden the chocolate. Use the remaining chocolate to brush another layer over the first and continue to chill or freeze until set.

Spoon about ¼ cup of the ice cream into each shell, smoothing the tops, and freeze for at least 2 hours or until firm.

Shortly before serving, whip the cream with the sugar and rum until stiff peaks form. Peel the paper liners very carefully away from the frozen filled chocolate shells and dollop or pipe the rum-flavored whipped cream over the ice cream. Arrange 1 or 2 filled shells on each dessert plate.

Yield: 4 to 8 servings

Iced Chocolate Cases filled with liqueurs and fresh fruit and Strawberries Almondine.

Blackberry Sorbet

Mrs. Flower was an old, aristocratic Anglo-Irish lady. Kathleen washes up for us. When Mrs. Flower died, she was saddened. "That's the last of the old royalties," she shouted to the young people in the kitchen, who didn't understand. The era was already gone.

Gone are the groups of gentry once found in the hotels, at the shows and races. Smart, jolly, and self-assured, they were terrifyingly intimidating if you were not one of them. Gone are so many of the houses they came from, their furniture, their books, and their beautiful walled gardens.

It was my lot to live on the fringes of this society. I sometimes received an invitation to one of the big houses. I particularly remember a June dinner party at one such house. The final course was a melting strawberry sorbet. At another, I remember a wonderful loin of perfect local lamb. It had been boned and stuffed with buttery crumbs and fresh herbs from the garden, then rolled up and tied for roasting. Tiny scones with fresh homemade jam and thick cream instead of butter and deep soft sponge cakes were served for afternoon tea. It was on rare visits to these houses that I found a new dimension in Irish cooking.

This sorbet can be made without an ice-cream machine, but if you have one do not hesitate to use it. If you use frozen fruit, put it straight into the hot syrup. The fruit will thaw and the syrup cool at the same time.

This recipe can also be used to make strawberry sorbet, using the same amount of strawberries as of the blackberries used here and mashing them with a fork so that the pulp is mushy but not puréed.

4   cups fresh blackberries
1   cup sugar
5   to 6 sweet unsprayed geranium leaves
    (optional)
½   to 1 tablespoon fresh lemon juice
2   large egg whites at room temperature

Purée the blackberries in a food processor and force them through a sieve into a bowl, pressing the pulp to remove the seeds. Reserve the fruit purée.

Combine the sugar with 1 cup water and the optional geranium leaves and bring to a boil in a

112

In September the local children bring us vast quantities of wild blackberries picked from the hedges for jams, tarts, and sorbets.

heavy saucepan. Boil for about 2 minutes, or until a candy thermometer registers 220° F. Let the syrup cool, then stir it into the reserved fruit purée with the lemon juice. (The mixture will seem quite sweet before it is frozen.)

Pour the fruit mixture into a shallow metal dish and freeze until almost set. Beat the egg whites until stiff peaks just form. In a bowl with an electric mixer beat the nearly frozen fruit mixture to a slush, then beat in the egg whites. Transfer the sorbet to the metal dish and freeze for several hours, or until nearly solid. Scoop or spoon the sorbet into stemmed glasses or dessert dishes.

Yield: about 6 servings

Iced Chocolate Oranges

❧

These desserts are lovely for a party. They are time-consuming to make, but they look very pretty when finished and decorated. The flesh is scooped out of the orange peels and made into orange ice cream, which is then spooned back into the empty orange shells along with a chocolate ice cream.

4   attractive, unblemished oranges
2   to 3 tablespoons sugar
1   recipe Vanilla Ice Cream (page 105),
       prepared up to the point of folding in the
       whipped cream
1   ounce semisweet chocolate, chopped
½   ounce unsweetened chocolate, chopped
1   teaspoon unflavored gelatin
Orange segments and/or whole fresh bay leaves
       (optional) for garnish

Cut a slice off the tops of the oranges. Using a small sharp knife or a grapefruit spoon and working over a bowl to catch the juices, carefully scoop out the pulp from the oranges, leaving a hollow shell. Put the shells in the freezer until ready to fill. Purée the pulp and juice in a blender or food processor and then force through a sieve, discarding the solids. Measure 1¼ cups of the orange juice, sweeten it to taste with the sugar, and reserve it. (If there is not enough juice, add extra to make 1¼ cups. If there is extra juice, save it for another use.)

Divide the Vanilla Ice Cream mousse between 2 bowls.

Melt the chocolates together in the top of a double boiler set over hot water, or in a low oven, or in a microwave oven. Let cool slightly, then stir in 1 of the bowls of Vanilla Ice Cream mousse. Fold in half of the whipped cream, divide the mixture among the prepared orange shells, filling each about half full, and freeze for a few minutes.

In a bowl soften the gelatin in 2 tablespoons of the measured orange juice and then warm gently, set in a pan of hot water, stirring, or in a microwave oven to dissolve the gelatin. Stir the dissolved gelatin mixture and the remaining 1⅛ cups orange into the second bowl of Vanilla Ice Cream mousse. Fold in the remaining whipped cream and divide among the prepared orange shells, covering the chocolate mixture. (There will probably be extra orange mixture. Freeze as for the Vanilla Ice Cream.) Return the orange shells, covered with plastic wrap, to the freezer for at least 4 hours or up to 24 hours, or until frozen solid. The desserts may be made 1 or 2 days in advance and kept frozen.

Using a sharp knife, cut the oranges into quarters. Arrange 2 or 3 quarters per person on dessert plates and garnish with the orange segments, optional fresh bay leaves, and small scoops of the extra frozen orange mousse, as desired.

Yield: about 6 servings

Trifle

It's a bit annoying when somebody refers to "a lady's wine" or "a man's book." When it comes to trifle, however, I must admit that men, *in particular*, become passionate.

I once heard three men arguing about how to make the one-and-only authentic trifle. Each man's grandmother had made the trifle of his life, and each made it differently.

One of them had a granny from Drogheda who made trifle with sponge cakes spread with raspberry jam, topped with tinned pears, and moistened with pear juice. These were covered with a layer of custard and another of cream. No decorations, no Sherry.

The East Cork granny of the second man dissolved jelly in the juice of tinned peaches or pears and poured this with Sherry over sponge cakes. She put the fruit between the layers and topped the lot with whipped cream. No custard, no decorations.

The third man's rather grand Yorkshire granny put ratafia biscuits, macaroons, and sponge cakes in layers in a bowl and moistened them with Sherry, fruit juice, and lemon curd. Custard and sometimes cream topped the bowl, and crystallized violets and roses were used for decoration.

Well, now I have my own grandsons, and this is how I make my trifle—with acknowledgments to my own granny. I use Jane Grigson's recipe for pastry cream, however, in place of the usual custard. It comes from her book *Good Things*.

1	recipe Mrs. Lamb's Sponge Cake (page 134), day old, or 1 pound bought sponge cake layers
1	to 1¼ cups raspberry jam or preserves
¾	cup Sherry
1	recipe Pastry Cream (page 122)
1¼	cups heavy cream, whipped
8	blanched and skinned almonds
8	glacéed cherries
8	sticks of angelica

Slice the cake layers horizontally with a serrated knife and cut into large pieces. If the raspberry jam is thick, thin it to a spreadable consistency with 1 or 2 tablespoons of the Sherry. Spread the jam over all the cut surfaces of the cake and arrange the cake pieces, jam sides up, in layers in a 2- to 2½-quart attractive glass serving bowl. The cake should come within 3 inches of the top of the bowl.

Drizzle the remaining Sherry over the cake, then spread with the pastry cream followed by the whipped cream. Halve or quarter the almonds and cherries, cut the angelica into thin 1-inch-long sticks, and use these to decorate the top of the trifle.

Chill the trifle, covered, for about 8 hours. To serve, spoon down through all of the layers.

Yield: 8 to 10 servings

Irish Apple Cake

—❧—

The west coast of Ireland is very bare and completely windswept. The grass is cropped short, burned by the salt winds. Thorn bushes are permanently bent away from the force of the Atlantic gales, and trees cannot exist. It is farmed, however, and here and there one finds a farmhouse that accommodates the traveler, offering kindness and hospitality in direct contrast to the severity of the climate.

In one of these farms a housekeeper named Mary cooks for three unmarried brothers, their widowed sister, and the guests. She never stops working. The house is filled with the smell of her bread, scones, and apple cakes. It is her apple cake recipe that follows.

Homemade apple cakes are *the* most popular sweet in Ireland. They are found on the table in every home. When apples are finished, rhubarb comes in and makes a welcome change for the cake's filling. Some people make stiff pastries resembling shortcrust, while others, like us, prefer a softer dough, difficult to handle but delicious. We serve the cake with softly whipped cream.

All the apple cakes are made with cooking, not eating, apples. Bramley's Seedlings, the most widely grown commercial variety at present, break down in the required way to a white foamy mass when cooked. Cut them into chunks. If they are meant to keep their shape as in an open apple tart, they should be sliced.

2   cups cake flour (not self-rising)
¾   teaspoon double-acting baking powder
1   stick (½ cup) cold unsalted butter, cut into pieces
½   cup plus 2 to 3 tablespoons sugar
2   extra-large eggs, 1 of them beaten with 1 tablespoon milk for a glaze
7   tablespoons cold milk
1   to 2 tart cooking apples (about ¾ pound), such as Rome Beauty or Granny Smith, peeled, cored, and cut into rough ¾-inch chunks
2   whole cloves (optional)

Lightly butter a 9-inch pie plate.

Sift the flour and baking powder together into a large bowl. Rub in the butter until the mixture resembles coarse meal. Stir in ½ cup of the sugar. Make a well in the center of the mixture and into it pour the unblended egg, beaten, and the milk all at once. Stir to make a very soft, wet, sticky dough that does not clean the sides of the bowl. Dip your hands into flour and then pat about half the dough into the prepared pie plate, covering the bottom and side.

Distribute the apple cubes over the dough to within ¾ inch of the edge and sprinkle them

116

Sheep grazing at Ballymaloe.

with the remaining 2 to 3 tablespoons sugar, depending upon the tartness of the apples. Stud with the cloves. Brush the edge of the dough with some of the glaze.

Sprinkle a large dinner plate generously with flour and pat the remaining dough onto the plate. Invert the plate and the dough over the apples in the pie plate, dropping the dough into place over the apples. (If the dough breaks, simply patch it and don't worry if it looks a bit raggedy.) Press the edges of the top and bottom crusts together with the tines of a fork, sealing the edge all around, and make a single slit in the top as a steam vent. Brush the top with the remaining glaze.

Bake the cake in the middle of a preheated 350° F. oven for 40 and 50 minutes, or until the dough is golden and the apples are tender and juicy when pierced with the tip of a knife. Serve warm.

Yield: 6 to 8 servings

Plum Pudding

The tradition that every member of the household who helped make the Christmas pudding could have a wish that was likely (note, never a firm promise) to come true was, of course, a ruse to get all the children to help with the heavy work of stirring it. I only discovered this after I was married and had to do the job myself. This recipe, multiplied many times, was made all at once. In a machineless age, mixing all those expensive ingredients properly was a formidable task. Our puddings were mixed in an enormous china crock that held the bread for the household during the rest of the year. My mother, nanny, and the cook stirred in turns, falling back with much panting and laughing after a few minutes' work. I don't think I was really much help to them.

Christmas puddings should be given at least six weeks to mature. They will keep for a year. They become richer and firmer with age but lose the lightness of the fruit flavor. We always eat our last plum pudding at Easter. If possible, prepare your own fresh beef suet—it is better than the packaged product.

1	*tart baking apple*
4	*cups soft fresh bread crumbs*
¾	*cup sugar*
3	*tablespoons all-purpose flour*
½	*teaspoon ground cinnamon*
¼	*teaspoon ground cloves*
¼	*teaspoon ground ginger*
⅛	*teaspoon salt*
1½	*cups (6 ounces) shredded beef suet*
1½	*cups currants*
1½	*cups raisins*
¾	*cup chopped candied fruit peel*
3	*extra-large eggs, beaten*
¼	*cup Irish whiskey*

Brandy Butter (page 119) or Whiskey Cream (page 119) as accompaniments (optional)

Core the apple and bake it in a dish with a small amount of water in a preheated 350° F. oven for about 30 minutes, or until softened. Let cool slightly, peel, and mash the flesh. You will need about ¼ cup mashed apple flesh.

Grease a 2-quart pudding mold or deep bowl.

In a large bowl stir together the bread crumbs, sugar, flour, cinnamon, cloves, ginger, and salt. Stir in the suet, currants, raisins, and candied fruit peel. In a small bowl stir together the eggs, whiskey, and apple, then add to the dry ingredients in the large bowl and stir until blended well.

Spoon the batter into the prepared mold or bowl and cover the surface directly with a round of greased parchment paper. Then cover the pudding mold with its tight-fitting lid. If using a bowl, cover it with a large round of heavy parchment or brown paper and secure the paper by tying it with kitchen string. Set the mold or bowl in a large kettle and fill the kettle one-third full of boiling water. Cover the kettle and simmer the pudding over low heat for 8 hours, or until firm. (Do not allow the water to boil over the top of the mold and do not let it boil dry either.)

Remove the mold or bowl from the kettle and let the pudding cool. Store the pudding for at least 6 weeks for proper maturing, either in the mold or unmolded and wrapped well. Serve hot with the optional Brandy Butter or Whiskey Cream.

Yield: 8 to 10 servings

Brandy Butter

❧

This is one of the traditional accompaniments to Plum Pudding.

7   tablespoons unsalted butter, softened
½   cup sugar
2   tablespoons brandy

Cream the butter and sugar together in a bowl until pale and fluffy. Beat in the brandy. Chill if not serving immediately. This may be made up to 2 days in advance and kept covered and chilled. Serve at room temperature.

Yield: about ¾ cup

Whiskey Cream

❧

This is an easy and delicious cream to serve with many of the Christmas desserts. It can also be served with coffee ice cream—in fact, it goes well with anything made of coffee.

1   cup heavy cream, chilled
1   tablespoon sugar
3   tablespoons Irish whiskey

Whip the cream with the sugar in a bowl until soft peaks form. Add the whiskey and continue beating until stiff peaks form. Serve chilled within an hour or so of making.

Yield: 2 cups

Overleaf: A bumper crop of wild damsons.

Pastry Cream

Use this pastry cream for the Trifle (page 115) or to fill tiny tart shells to serve for tea or on a petits fours tray. It can also be used in Iced Chocolate Cases with Rum Cream (page 111)—in which case, top with sliced strawberries macerated in a little sugar and Kirsch.

1½   cups milk
1   small vanilla bean, halved lengthwise, or ½ teaspoon vanilla extract
2   extra-large eggs
½   cup sugar
¼   cup all-purpose flour

In a heavy saucepan scald the milk with the vanilla bean. (Do not add the extract, if using, at this point.) Separate 1 of the eggs and in a bowl whisk together the yolk and the remaining whole egg, reserving the separated white. Whisk in the sugar and flour and add the hot milk in a thin stream, whisking constantly and reserving the vanilla bean, if using. Transfer the mixture to the pan and cook over low heat, stirring constantly, for 5 to 8 minutes, or until the mixture is thickened and just comes to a boil. Strain the custard through a sieve into a bowl. Scrape the seeds from the vanilla bean, if using, into the custard or add the vanilla extract and let cool to room temperature. Beat the reserved egg white until it holds stiff, but not dry, peaks and fold it into the custard. Use the pastry cream immediately or chill, covered, until ready to use. The pastry cream should be very thick but spreadable. If it seems too thick, thin with about 1 tablespoon hot water.

Yield: 1¾ to 2 cups

Strawberry Almondine Petits Fours

———— ❧ ————

Strawberry Almondine Petits Fours are among the prettiest and freshest of all. One needs to be careful and fairly experienced in handling the fragile ingredients. Prepare them in a moment when you are feeling like an artist rather than "a cook in a rush." Be sure to roll the paste into a thin, even layer. Do not keep them more than 6 or 7 hours, or the juices will begin to run and make a mess of your pretty dish.

12   *fresh strawberries*
½   *cup (about 2 ounces) angelica*
1½   *cups blanched and skinned almonds*
1   *cup less 1 tablespoon sugar plus additional for sprinkling the board*
1   *to 2 lightly beaten egg whites*
36   *to 48 paper or foil petits fours cases*

Hull the strawberries and pat them thoroughly dry. Cut enough of the angelica to make 24 small stick shapes to resemble strawberry stems. Mince the remaining angelica.

Grind the almonds with the sugar in batches in a food processor or blender. (The almonds should be ground fine but not be oily.) Blend in the chopped angelica and enough of the egg white to make a paste that holds together but is not overly sticky. Let the mixture stand for about 15 minutes.

Sprinkle a cutting board or other work surface with a little granulated sugar. Divide the almond mixture into 12 portions and flatten each on the sugared board to form a round about ⅛ inch thick and large enough to encase a whole strawberry. Center 1 strawberry on each round and fold the almond mixture around it to encase it completely. The berries may be prepared up to this point 2 hours in advance. Set aside in a cool place or chilled.

No more than 1 hour before serving, with a sharp knife cut each berry in half lengthwise. Insert 1 angelica stick in each stem end and arrange in the petits fours cases.

Yield: 24 petits fours

123

Shortcrust Pastry

———— ✿ ————

This is used for the Mince Pies (page 126) as well as for decorations for the Hot Cross Buns (page 144). It is also a nice, rich pastry for all manner of fruit tarts.

2 cups all-purpose flour
1 tablespoon confectioners' sugar
½ teaspoon salt
1½ sticks (¾ cup) cold unsalted butter, cut into pieces
1 extra-large egg yolk, beaten with enough cold water to make 3 tablespoons

Combine the flour, sugar, and salt in a large bowl and rub in the butter until the mixture resembles coarse meal. Add the egg mixture and toss with a fork until the dough can be gathered into a ball. If the dough seems too dry, sprinkle with an additional 1 to 2 teaspoons water, a few drops at a time. (The dough can also be made in a food processor, following the same sequence.)

Halve the dough and on a lightly floured board pat each portion into a thick disk. Chill the dough, wrapped well, for at least 30 minutes or up to 24 hours. The dough keeps, frozen, for 1 month.

Yield: about 1 pound pastry, or enough to make thirty 2½- to 3-inch tartlets or one 9-inch double-crust pie

Making a fruit tart.

The farm workers' tea house.

Mince Pies

— ❧ —

This is an old family recipe. The mincemeat should be made in November for Christmas. The pies may be cooked in shells made of puff or flaky pastry or rich shortcrust and served with a sweetened cream flavored with whiskey or with some whiskey poured through the slit on the top. My mother ate them with a little neat Irish whiskey poured into them; we were always intrigued by the way she carefully measured the whiskey through a fork. Though these are always served as tartlets at Ballymaloe, the amounts of mincemeat and pastry are right for making a 9-inch American-style double-crust pie, too.

1   *tart baking apple, such as Rome Beauty or Cortland*
1   *large lemon*
1½ *cups raisins*
¾   *cup sultanas (golden raisins)*
¾   *cup currants*
⅓   *cup mixed candied citrus peel*
2   *cups (about ½ pound) finely chopped suet*
2   *cups packed light brown sugar*
1   *tablespoon orange marmalade*
⅓   *cup whiskey*
1   *recipe Shortcrust Pastry (page 124)*
1   *large egg, beaten with ¼ teaspoon salt for glaze*
Whipped cream, Whiskey Cream (page 119), or Irish whiskey as accompaniments (optional)

Core and peel the apple, combine it with several tablespoons water in a shallow baking dish, and bake it, covered loosely, in a preheated 350° F. oven until fork-tender. Let cool slightly, peel, and mash.

Grate fine the lemon's rind, squeeze the juice, and combine both with the mashed apple, the raisins, sultanas, currants, candied citrus peel, suet, brown sugar, marmalade, and ½ cup water in a large bowl. Stir with a wooden spoon until blended well. Simmer the mixture in a heavy 3-quart non-reactive saucepan over low heat, stirring often, for 30 minutes. Stir in the whiskey, let the mincemeat cool to room temperature, and chill it, covered, for 2 weeks. The mincemeat may be frozen for 1 year.

When ready to bake the pies, grease about fifteen to twenty 2½-inch tartlet molds or 2 large baking sheets. Halve the shortcrust pastry and reserve one piece, chilled. Roll out the other piece ⅛ inch thick on a lightly floured surface and, using a 2½- to 3-inch round cutter, cut out rounds, rerolling and cutting the scraps. Press them gently into the tartlet molds or arrange them on the baking sheets. Spoon about 2 teaspoons of the mincemeat onto the center of each round, reserving the remaining mincemeat, covered and chilled or frozen, then brush the edges with some of the glaze. Roll and cut out the remaining dough in the same way, top the pies with the rounds, and press the edges together with the tines of a fork, sealing them. Make a small steam slit in the top of each pie with a sharp knife. Brush the top crusts with the remaining glaze.

Bake the pies in the middle of a preheated 400° F. oven for about 15 minutes, or until the pastry is golden and crisp. Transfer the pies to a rack and let them cool. Serve slightly warm or at room temperature.

Yield: 15 to 20 mince pies (about 4 cups mincemeat, including leftovers)

Rhubarb Almond Tart

❧

The crust for this tart is more like a confection than a pastry; as it cooks it actually caramelizes. Fill the crust with the rhubarb only shortly before serving, so that it will remain crisp. The tart can also be made into tartlets, using 2½-inch molds, preferably with removable rims. If you wish, raspberries, grapes, or sliced peaches may be substituted for the poached rhubarb.

FOR THE FILLING
1   *cup sugar*
¾   *pound fresh rhubarb (about 2 plump red stalks), cut into 1-inch pieces*
FOR THE CRUST
¾   *stick (6 tablespoons) unsalted butter, softened*
7   *tablespoons sugar*
1   *cup ground almonds (see Note)*

¾   *cup heavy cream*

To make the filling, combine the sugar with 1 cup water in a heavy non-reactive saucepan and bring to a boil over medium heat, stirring constantly until the sugar is dissolved. Add the rhubarb and simmer for 4 to 6 minutes, or until the rhubarb is softened but still holds its shape. Transfer the rhubarb to a bowl with a slotted spoon and let it cool.

To make the crust, beat the butter, sugar, and almonds together in a bowl until the mixture forms a smooth paste. Lightly flour your hands, then pat the almond paste (it will be sticky) evenly onto the bottom and side of a 10-inch round or two 6-inch round tart pans with removable rims. Bake the crust in the middle of a preheated 350° F. oven for 8 to 12 minutes, or until it is bubbling and a rich golden brown. (Do not let the crust burn; watch it carefully as it bakes from 8 minutes on.) Let cool completely.

No more than 1 hour before serving, arrange the rhubarb over the crust. Just before serving, pipe or dollop the whipped cream around the edge of the tart.

Yield: about 10 servings

Note: To grind almonds, use a nut or spice grinder or a food processor. If using a food processor, grind with about 1 tablespoon flour and process in short bursts so that the nuts are uniformly ground almost to a powder but do not become oily.

Balloons
(Sugared Doughnuts)

Balloons are a very cheap and simple doughnut. I sometimes cook them for the children on Sundays. They were a delight in my childhood, when my mother cooked them for me. As she made them, she would share with me her memories of her early married days in Cambridge during the First World War—of food queues, old friends I did not know, and bed-sitter parties where a feast was a feed of balloons.

1 cup all-purpose flour
1 tablespoon sugar plus additional for coating
   the doughnuts
1 teaspoon double-acting baking powder
About ½ cup milk
Vegetable oil for deep-frying the doughnuts

Sift the flour, 1 tablespoon of the sugar, and the baking powder into a bowl and slowly whisk in enough of the milk to make a very soft dough that can be dropped from a spoon. Heat 2 to 3 inches of the oil to 370° F. in a deep-fryer or a deep saucepan. Spoon out rounded tablespoons of the dough, lower them near the oil's surface, and push them off into the hot oil so that they drop in fairly round balls. (It is not necessary that the shapes be perfect—in fact, it is more interesting if they are not.) Fry the doughnuts in batches, turning them carefully with a slotted spoon, for about 4 minutes, or until all sides are golden brown and the balloons are puffed. Remove with a slotted spoon and drain on paper towels. While still hot, roll the balloons in the additional granulated sugar.

Serve warm.

Yield: about 18

Guests and grandchildren meet at children's tea, and on special days I make Balloons for them.

Apples in Irish Mist

——— ❧ ———

My favorite apple tree was about twenty feet high. It had lanky, unpruned, lichen-covered branches and bright red apples. They were tempting to look at but dreadful to eat. Their one virtue was that they stewed to a beautiful fluffy pink mass. Nobody else liked the tree, and one day it was cut down when I was not around to protect it. I have never had pink stewed apples since.

Apples that I love are always disappearing. In mid-August we had the red-striped Beauty of Bath — the first delicious eating apples of the season. A fortnight later came creamy Miller's Seedlings, wonderfully crisp and juicy apples. Next came Worcester Pearmains, bright red and not bad to eat. Laxton's Superbs, Cox's Orange Pippins, and Russets followed.

On November evenings, my father would select an enormous Charles Ross in perfect condition. Too big for one person, it was solemnly shared as we sat around the fire.

There are hundreds of different varieties of apple, each with its own distinctive characteristics, like the wines of France. Nowadays apple trees, like hens and humans, have to produce with maximum efficiency. The subtler virtues no longer pay.

The recipe below will be good made with Golden Delicious, but better with one of the old-fashioned eating apples.

8   *eating apples such as Golden Delicious*
¾   *cup sugar*
2   *tablespoons fresh lemon juice*
3   *tablespoons Irish Mist liqueur*

Peel, quarter, and slice the apples between ⅛ and ¼ inch thick and in a non-reactive saucepan combine them with the sugar and lemon juice, stirring to blend. Simmer the mixture, covered tightly, over very low heat for 15 to 20 minutes, or until the apples are tender but not broken and mushy. (Remove the lid during the last few minutes of cooking to let any excess liquid evaporate.) Let cool, then stir in the liqueur.

Yield: 6 to 8 servings

Jane's Shortbread Cookies

This shortbread mixture makes a good biscuit to go with morning coffee or fruit fools. It was first made for us by one of my children's friends when I decided to let them all loose in the kitchen on a wet Sunday afternoon. No wonder that I always so firmly believe in having children in the kitchen . . . well, almost always!

1¼   cups all-purpose flour
⅓   cup sugar
1   stick (½ cup) cold unsalted butter, cut into pieces

Combine the flour and sugar in a bowl and rub in the butter until the mixture resembles coarse meal. On a lightly floured surface knead the mixture until it forms a smooth dough. Roll it out slightly less than ¼ inch thick and, using a 2½-inch round cutter, cut out as many rounds as possible, rerolling the scraps and cutting out more rounds.

On ungreased baking sheets arrange the rounds about 1 inch apart and bake them in the middle of a preheated 350° F. oven for 12 to 15 minutes, or until the bottoms are golden. Transfer the cookies to racks and let them cool. The cookies keep in a covered tin for about 3 days, or frozen for 1 month.

Yield: 18 to 22 cookies

Note: We also make this recipe for strawberry shortcake, rolling the dough into larger rounds and sandwiching whipped cream and sliced sweetened strawberries between them.

Gingersnaps

One of the great treats of my childhood was to picnic at a rocky cove on the coast of Cork on a hot summer day. We usually sheltered under the walls of an abandoned cottage on a grassy cliff.

My mother would first unpack raw, well-scrubbed potatoes, a saucepan, and a spirit stove. We would bring her a bucket full of sea water, and she would proceed to cook the potatoes in it. In half an hour we would be wet and shivering from our swim, and ready to do justice to those marvelous potatoes, served with big pats of butter. Cold chicken, ham, brawn (meat from a boiled pig's head, spiced and pressed), and old-fashioned salads of very crisp lettuce with slices of egg and tomato and lashings of salad cream—all emerged from the picnic basket. Fresh fruit followed.

At 4:30 it was time to find a well and to bring my mother fresh spring water to boil for the tea, while we had our last swim of the day. Tea was taken with freshly buttered slices of barm brack (a fruit loaf specialty from County Cork), perhaps biscuits and cake as well. Then we rumbled home along the dusty roads, we children singing in the back of the car at the tops of our voices. Country girls passed by in brightly colored satin dresses, bound for an evening's dancing on the boards at the crossroads. We begged to stop and wait to see the dancing, but children had to go to bed early.

This gingersnap recipe might suit somebody small, wet, and shivery on a windy strand. If they are not eaten the same day they're baked, store them, wrapped in plastic wrap, in airtight containers.

2	cups all-purpose flour
1	teaspoon ground ginger
½	teaspoon baking soda
½	teaspoon salt
1	stick (½ cup) unsalted butter, softened
¾	cup firmly packed light brown sugar
1	extra-large egg
½	cup dark molasses or black treacle

Grated rind of 1 orange (optional)

⅓	cup chopped nuts (optional)
⅓	cup raisins (optional)

In a bowl sift together the flour, ginger, baking soda, and salt. In a large bowl with an electric mixer cream the butter with the brown sugar until fluffy. Beat in the egg and molasses until blended well. Stir in the flour mixture until blended and then the orange, nuts, and raisins.

Drop the batter 2 inches apart by teaspoonfuls onto greased baking sheets and bake in a preheated 350° F. oven for 10 to 14 minutes, or until the cookies are firm to the touch. Transfer to racks and let cool completely.

Yield: about 3 dozen cookies

Brown Picnic Cookies

These are rich with butter, but not too sweet, and are a lovely accompaniment to fruit eaten out of hand on a picnic.

¾ cup all-purpose flour
¾ cup whole-wheat flour
1 stick (½ cup) cold unsalted butter, cut into pieces
2 tablespoons light brown sugar
2 tablespoons Lyle's Golden Syrup or honey

Combine the flours in a bowl and rub in the butter until the mixture resembles coarse meal. Stir in the brown sugar and syrup. Gather the dough into a ball, then knead it on a lightly floured surface for 1 to 2 minutes, or until it is smooth. Roll out ¼ inch thick, cut into 1- by 2-inch rectangles, and arrange 1 inch apart on ungreased baking sheets. Bake the cookies in the middle of a preheated 325° F. oven for about 20 minutes, or until lightly browned. Transfer to racks and let cool.

Yield: about 20 cookies

Mrs. Lamb's Sponge Cake

Young trainees can make disastrous mistakes. When one occurs, I try to be patient and to remember my early days, when I destroyed so many precious ingredients in wartime—fortunately they were my own. One year I burned three Christmas cakes before taking one out of the oven in time. On another occasion I beat sixteen eggs with their equal weight in sugar by hand for a whole day in an effort to achieve the smooth mousse-like texture that I had been taught was the correct basis for a sponge cake. It never happened, and the result was finally fed to the chickens. Good came out of this episode in the end, however, when a friend, Mrs. Lamb, came to my rescue with a more reliable recipe. This cake is made in two layers, which are sandwiched together with cream and fresh fruit or preserves. It is especially good with a fresh strawberry filling. Any leftover cake can be used for Trifle (page 115). To make chocolate sponge cake, reduce the flour by ¼ cup and add ¼ cup unsweetened cocoa powder.

1¼   *cups cake flour (not self-rising)*
1¼   *teaspoon double-acting baking powder*
3   *extra-large eggs, separated*
1¼   *cups sugar*

Sift the cake flour with the baking powder into a bowl. In a bowl with an electric mixer beat the yolks with the sugar for about 3 minutes, or until the mixture is very light. Beat in ⅓ cup warm water, then continue to beat for about 10 minutes, or until very light, fluffy, thickened, and creamy. Fold in the flour mixture gently but thoroughly. Beat the egg whites in another bowl until they hold stiff, but not dry, peaks. Stir about one fourth of the whites into the yolk mixture, then gently fold in the remainder.

Divide the batter between 2 buttered and floured 8-inch round cake pans, smoothing the tops. Bake the sponge cakes in the middle of a preheated 375° F. oven for 18 to 20 minutes, or until the tops are light golden brown and the cakes pull away from the sides of the pans. Let the cakes cool in the pans on racks for about 5 minutes, then turn out of the pans and let cool completely on the racks. The cakes may be used immediately or wrapped and frozen for up to 1 month.

Yield: two 8-inch layers

Chocolate Cake with Chocolate Icing

This rich chocolate layer cake is our standard recipe for children's birthday parties.

FOR THE CAKE

2	cups cake flour (not self-rising)
½	cup unsweetened alkalized cocoa powder (preferably Droste's)
1½	teaspoons double-acting baking powder
4	ounces semisweet chocolate, grated
2¼	sticks (1 cup plus 2 tablespoons) unsalted butter, softened
1¼	cups sugar
4	extra-large eggs
1	teaspoon vanilla extract
½	cup milk

FOR THE ICING

6	ounces semisweet chocolate
½	stick (¼ cup) unsalted butter, softened
2	extra-large eggs, beaten lightly

Butter a 9-inch round cake pan, at least 2 inches deep, or a 9-inch springform pan. Line the bottom of the pan with a buttered round of wax paper (or butter-wrapper papers) and sprinkle with flour, tapping out the excess.

To make the cake, sift the cake flour with the cocoa powder, baking powder, and a pinch of salt into a bowl. Stir in the grated chocolate and set aside. In a bowl with an electric mixer cream the butter with the sugar until light and fluffy. Beat in the eggs, one at a time, beating well after each addition. With the mixer at low speed, beat in the flour mixture alternately with the vanilla and milk until the batter is combined well.

Pour the batter into the prepared pan, smoothing the top, and bake in the middle of a preheated 350° F. oven for 50 to 60 minutes, or until a tester inserted in the center comes out clean and the cake has begun to pull away from the side of the pan. Let the cake cool in the pan on a rack for 10 minutes, then turn out of the pan and let cool completely on the rack.

To make the icing, melt the chocolate with 2 tablespoons water in the top of a double boiler set over hot water, or put the pan in the warm oven for a few minutes to melt the chocolate. Off the heat, beat in the butter, then the eggs, until the mixture is smooth and shiny. Let the icing cool until thick enough to spread. (If necessary, the icing can be chilled for a few minutes to speed the thickening, but watch carefully so that it does not become too thick.)

With a serrated knife slice the cake layer in half horizontally. Use half of the icing as a filling between the layers, then frost the top of the cake with the remaining icing. (The side of this cake is not frosted.) Let the cake set for about 1 hour before cutting.

Yield: one 9-inch layer cake, serving about 12

Christmas Cake

—— ❧ ——

This Christmas Cake is rich and moist; the cake keeps until Easter, I can tell you that, but there my experiments have always ended!

Make it four to six weeks before Christmas. Keep in an airtight tin or a plastic bag in a larder or unheated room until about twelve days before Christmas.

Put on the almond icing twelve days before Christmas. Leave it to set for a day before putting on the royal icing, and for another day before adding piped decoration. (Stuck-on decorations such as fir trees and snowmen are put on immediately, while the icing is soft.) The simplest way to control the texture of the icing is in storage. If you keep it in a damp larder it will stay soft—so soft it can run right off the cake in wet weather. If you want it hard and dry, keep it in a warm dry place.

FOR THE CAKE

2	cups cake flour (not self-rising)
2¼	sticks (1 cup plus 2 tablespoons) unsalted butter, softened
1	cup sugar
4	extra-large eggs
⅓	cup whiskey, rum, or brandy
2	teaspoons grated orange rind
1	teaspoon grated lemon rind
1½	cups currants
1½	cups sultanas (golden raisins)
¾	cup raisins
¾	cup chopped glacéed cherries
½	cup chopped candied citrus peel
½	cup coarsely chopped blanched and skinned almonds

FOR THE ALMOND ICING

1	extra-large egg
1	teaspoon whiskey
½	teaspoon fresh lemon juice
2	cups ground almonds (see Note)
2	cups confectioners' sugar
1	cup granulated sugar

FOR THE ROYAL ICING

2	extra-large egg whites
2	tablespoons fresh lemon juice
3½	cups confectioners' sugar
1	extra-large egg white, beaten until frothy

Butter a 9-inch round cake pan, at least 3 inches deep, or a 9-inch springform pan. Line the bottom of the pan with a round of buttered waxed paper (or butter-wrapper papers). Make a collar around the pan by wrapping it in a sheet of wax paper that extends about 2 inches above the side and tying the paper in place with string, as if making a collar for a soufflé.

To make the cake, sift the flour and set aside. In a bowl with an electric mixer cream the butter with the sugar until the mixture is light and fluffy. Beat in the eggs, one at a time, beating well after each addition. With the mixer at low speed, beat in the flour alternately with the whiskey until blended. Beat in the orange and lemon rinds. Stir in the currants, sultanas, rai-

Trifle, Christmas Cake, and Plum Pudding in front of the drawing room fire.

sins, glacéed cherries, candied peel, and almonds until the batter is blended well.

Turn the mixture into the prepared pan and bake the cake in the middle of a preheated 300° F. oven for about 3 hours, or until it is firm to the touch and golden and a tester inserted in the center comes out clean. Let the cake cool on a rack in the pan for about 15 minutes, then remove the collar, turn the cake out of the pan, remove the wax paper liner, and let the cake cool completely on the rack. The cake may be served immediately or kept, covered and chilled, for up to 2 months.

To make the almond icing, whisk together the egg, whiskey, and lemon juice in a bowl. Add the almonds, confectioners' sugar, and granulated sugar and work the mixture into a smooth paste.

(This can be done by hand, in an electric mixer with a paddle, or in a food processor.) Pat the mixture into a disk, wrap it in plastic wrap, and chill it for about 1 hour.

To make the royal icing, in a bowl with an electric mixer beat the egg whites with the lemon juice until frothy. Add the confectioners' sugar and beat for 5 to 7 minutes, or until the whites are very fluffy and hold soft peaks. (If the icing is not to be used right away, keep the bowl covered with a damp cloth or the whites will harden.)

Roll out the almond icing on a baking sheet or wooden board sprinkled with confectioners' sugar, forming a 13-inch round, about ½ inch thick. Brush the top of cake with the beaten egg white and invert the cake into the center of the almond icing circle. Lift the baking sheet and invert the cake onto a plate, turning it right side up and with the almond icing and baking sheet on top. Remove the baking sheet and pat the almond icing snugly around the side of the cake, trimming it even with the bottom. (Use scraps to patch any holes or cracks.) Let stand, uncovered, for at least 4 hours to set.

Frost with the royal icing, reserving some to pipe through a pastry bag fitted with a decorative tip. Let stand about 1 hour to set the royal icing.

Yield: one 9-inch cake, serving 20 to 24

Note: To grind almonds, use a nut or spice grinder or a food processor. If using a food processor, grind with about 1 tablespoon of the flour from the recipe and process in short bursts so that the nuts are uniformly ground almost to a powder but do not become oily.

Irish Brown Soda Bread

———— ❧ ————

I was many years married before I first triumphantly put a really good brown soda loaf on the tea table. Of course, this brought me no praise, only a few disillusioned grunts about the pity it was that I had taken so long to learn the art!

Yeast bread, cakes, pastry—anything had been to me easier than the elusive national loaf. Every woman I knew who made good bread appeared just to have "the touch." Some swore by kneading, others by never kneading; some put in half white flour, some none, and of course nobody ever went by standard measures—and neither did I in the end.

3¼ cups whole-wheat flour (preferably stone-ground)
1¼ cups all-purpose flour
2 teaspoons salt
1½ teaspoons baking soda
½ cup less 1 tablespoon quick-cooking or regular oats (not instant)
About 2½ cups buttermilk or sour milk (see Note)

Sift the flours, salt, and baking soda together into a large bowl. Stir in the oats. Make a well in the center, pour in the buttermilk, and stir with a wooden spoon until the mixture comes together to form a soft, moist dough. (If it seems too dry, add a few more tablespoons buttermilk.)

Turn the dough out onto a lightly floured surface and form it into a large, rounded disk, about 8 inches in diameter, and with a sharp knife cut a deep cross through the dough, cutting the disk almost into quarters. On a buttered baking sheet bake the bread in the middle of a preheated 425° F. oven for 15 minutes, then reduce the oven temperature to 350° F. and bake 20 to 25 minutes more, or until the bread is crusty and richly browned. Let it cool on a rack.

Yield: 1 large loaf

Note: To sour 2½ cups milk, in a bowl combine 1 tablespoon fresh lemon juice or vinegar with the milk and let stand for 10 to 15 minutes, or until thickened and curdled.

Ballymaloe breads for breakfast: Scones, Brown Soda Bread, and Brown Bread.

Ballymaloe Brown Bread

———— ❧ ————

This is really a stiff batter rather than a dough that can be kneaded. Loaves are made at least once daily at Ballymaloe. In our cool kitchen, we heat the flour and the mixing bowl in a low oven before making the bread, but most American kitchens are warm enough to omit this step.

3½   cups whole-wheat flour (preferably stone-ground)
¼   cup all-purpose flour
2   teaspoons salt
1½   packages active dry yeast
2   tablespoons molasses or black treacle

In a large bowl stir together the flours and salt. In a small bowl combine the yeast and molasses in ½ cup lukewarm water and let proof for 5 to 10 minutes.

Pour the yeast mixture and 1½ cups more lukewarm water into the dry ingredients and blend with a wooden spoon to make a thick, sticky dough. (If necessary, add up to ¼ cup more water.) Turn into a buttered loaf pan, 9 by 5 by 3 inches. Cover lightly with a tea towel and set aside to rise for 20 to 30 minutes, or until the dough nearly reaches the top of the loaf pan. Bake in the middle of a preheated 450° F. oven for 10 minutes, then reduce the heat to 425° F. and bake 35 to 40 minutes more, or until the top is richly browned and the loaf sounds hollow when tapped. Turn out onto a rack and let cool completely before slicing.

Yield: 1 loaf

Scones

❧

Scones are the first cousins of traditional Irish soda bread, and making them can be the first step in learning how to make the bigger loaf. Gentle handling is the secret. One does not knead in the normal way that is used for yeast bread. Just a quick light turning and folding in a sprinkling of flour are all that one needs to do. They are eaten for tea, split open and spread with butter and jam. At Ballymaloe we serve hot, freshly baked scones for breakfast.

2	cups all-purpose flour
1½	teaspoons sugar (optional)
½	teaspoon baking soda
¼	teaspoon salt
½	stick (¼ cup) cold unsalted butter, cut into pieces
¾	cup chilled buttermilk or sour milk (see Note)

Sift the flour, the optional sugar, baking soda, and salt into a bowl. Rub in the butter until the mixture resembles coarse meal. Stir in the buttermilk all at once and mix with a spoon until all ingredients are moistened and a dough forms. Turn out onto a lightly floured surface and knead 4 or 5 times. Roll or pat the dough ½ to ¾ inch thick and cut out rounds with a 2-inch cutter, or diamonds approximately the same size, re-forming and recutting the scraps. Arrange the scones 2 inches apart on an ungreased baking sheet. Bake the scones in the middle of a preheated 400° F. oven for 13 to 16 minutes, or until they are well risen and the tops are golden brown. Let the scones cool slightly on a rack, but serve them warm.

Yield: about 12 scones

Note: To sour ¾ cup milk, combine 1 teaspoon fresh lemon juice or vinegar with the milk and let stand for 10 to 15 minutes, or until thickened and curdled.

Hot Cross Buns

We eat Hot Cross Buns on Ash Wednesday and Good Friday, just twice a year. Compared to our other breads, they take so long to rise that I have almost missed the occasions to serve them once or twice. Now we start to make them early in the morning on the day we want them.

I usually make up my own mixture of freshly ground spices. "Mixed spice" is, however, sold in small packets in Irish shops and supermarkets at all times of the year. It consists of varying amounts of cinnamon, cloves, nutmeg, ginger, and mace.

1   package of active dry yeast
2   tablespoons plus 1 teaspoon sugar
1   cup milk
½   stick (¼ cup) unsalted butter, cut in pieces
3½   cups all-purpose flour
½   teaspoon salt
½   teaspoon ground cinnamon
¼   teaspoon ground cloves
¼   teaspoon ground nutmeg
1   extra-large egg, beaten lightly
¾   cup currants
¾   cup sultanas (golden raisins)

FOR THE DECORATION
½   recipe Shortcrust Pastry (page 124) or ½
     pound flaky pastry or puff pastry scraps
1   tablespoon sugar
1   tablespoon milk

Dissolve the yeast in a bowl with ¼ cup lukewarm water and 1 teaspoon of the sugar and let proof 5 to 10 minutes. Heat the milk in a saucepan with the butter until just lukewarm (the butter does not need to melt completely). Sift the flour, the salt, cinnamon, cloves, nutmeg, and 2 tablespoons of sugar into a large bowl, make a well in the center, and add the yeast mixture, milk mixture, and egg. Beat well to make a soft dough that can be kneaded. Turn onto a lightly floured surface and knead in the currants and sultanas, kneading for about 8 minutes, or until the dough is smooth and elastic. (This can also be done in an electric mixer with a dough hook.)

Turn the dough into a greased bowl, turning it to coat the top. Cover loosely with a tea towel and let rise in a warm place for 1 to 1½ hours, or until doubled in bulk.

To make the decorations, roll the pastry out about ⅛ inch thick on a lightly floured surface. Cut into strips about ⅜ inch wide and then cut each strip into 2-inch pieces. (You will need 32 pieces in all.) Dissolve the sugar in the milk in a small bowl.

When the dough has risen, punch it down, divide it into 16 pieces, and roll each piece into a ball. Arrange the balls 2 inches apart on greased baking sheets and brush them gently with the milk and sugar mixture. Make a cross with 2 strips of pastry on top of each ball, cover loosely with a tea towel, and set aside in a warm place for 20 to 30 minutes, or until nearly doubled in bulk.

Bake the rolls in the middle of a preheated 450° F. oven for 5 minutes. Reduce the oven temperature to 425° F. and bake the rolls for 10 to 15 minutes more, or until the buns are golden brown and the pastry trim is crisp. Transfer the buns to a rack and let them cool slightly. Serve warm. (Uneaten buns may be frozen and reheated in a low oven.)

Yield: 16 buns

A resting place on a walk in the woods.

DRINKS

Scalteen

---✤---

A rare account of everyday life in Ireland in the early nineteenth century was written by a Kilkenny school teacher in the 1830s, ten to fifteen years before the potato famine. The teacher was a great friend of the parish priest, and he describes his table in terms that resemble Maupassant's in his accounts of food in provincial France in the same century.

"We had two fine fat trout that were sweet too, and substantial. One of them as large as a small salmon. Then followed hard-boiled hen eggs and bruised asparagus, swimming in butter, laid out on fresh whipped cream and salt. Port wine and scaltin to drink."*

After all that food and Port wine, the scalteen must have afforded a sweet soporific dessert and drink combined: a comforting way to end a meal after a strenuous day.

1   to 2 teaspoons honey
2   tablespoons (1 ounce) Irish whiskey
½   cup hot milk

Blend the honey and whiskey together and stir the mixture into hot milk.

Yield: 1 serving

Cin Lae Amhaoibh, by Tomas de Bhaldraithe (*The Diaries of Humphry O'Sullivan*). Rights held by The Mercier Press, Cork.

Punch

---✤---

This is a delicious, warming drink. It is taken to cure colds, and many people are sure it does. It is certainly cheering! Have it at night, before getting into a warm bed.

¼   cup (2 ounces) Irish whiskey
1   tablespoon sugar
1   thick slice lemon
10   whole cloves

In a tall, heatproof glass or mug, stir together the whiskey and sugar. Stick the lemon slice with the cloves and add to the glass. Fill to the top with boiling water and serve immediately.

Yield: 1 serving

Conversion Chart

———— ❧ ————

American cooks measure most dry ingredients by volume rather than weight, using sets of standard measuring cups and spoons. This may seem confusing and impracticable to a British cook, who is used to weighing dry ingredients, but in fact it does work quite well. American cup and spoon measures are available in Britain, but you can just as easily use an ordinary measuring jug, which has millilitre and fluid ounce markings, and standard metric spoon measures.

The chart below gives the metric and imperial equivalents for American cup and spoon measures. Put the dry ingredient into the jug and shake it or tap it on the work surface to level it out. Check the quantity at eye level. For spoon measures, level off the ingredient by scraping with a knife.

The same cup and spoon measurements are used for liquid ingredients, so again follow the chart for equivalents.

BUTTER

Some confusion may arise over the measuring of butter and other hard fats. In the United States, butter is generally sold in a one-pound package, which contains four equal 'sticks.' The wrapper on each stick is marked to show tablespoons, so the cook can cut the stick according to the quantity required. The equivalent weights are:

1 stick = 115g/4oz
1 tablespoon = 15g/½oz

EGGS

American eggs are graded slightly differently than British eggs. Here are the equivalent sizes:

extra large egg (64g) = size 2 (65g)
large egg (57g) = size 3 (60g) or 4 (55g)
medium egg (50g) = size 5 (50g)

FLOUR

American all-purpose flour is milled from a mixture of hard and soft wheats, whereas British plain flour is made mainly from soft wheat. To achieve a near equivalent to American all-purpose flour, use half British plain flour and half strong bread flour.

American cake flour is made from soft wheat and can be replaced by British plain flour alone.

SUGAR

In the recipes in this book, if sugar is called for it is assumed to be granulated (unless otherwise specified). American granulated sugar is finer than British granulated, closer to caster sugar, so British cooks should use caster sugar throughout.

YEAST AND GELATINE

Quantities of dried yeast (called active dry yeast in the United States) are usually given in number of packages. Each of these packages contains 7g/¼oz yeast, which is equivalent to a scant tablespoon.

Quantities of unflavoured powdered gelatine are usually given in envelopes, each of which contains 7g/¼oz (about 1 tablespoon).

INGREDIENTS AND EQUIPMENT GLOSSARY

British English and American English are not always the same, particularly in the kitchen. The following ingredients and equipment used in this book are pretty much the same on both sides of the Atlantic, but just have different names.

AMERICAN	BRITISH
baking soda	bicarbonate of soda
bell pepper	sweet pepper (capsicum)
confectioners' sugar	icing sugar
Dutch oven	large flameproof casserole
half-and-half (11.7% fat)	half cream (12% fat)
heavy cream (37.6% fat)	whipping cream (35–40% fat)
jelly-roll pan	Swiss roll tin
kettle	very large saucepan
light cream (20.6% fat)	single cream (18% fat)
meat grinder	mincer
pastry bag	piping bag
pearl onion	button or baby onion
plastic wrap	cling film
scallion	spring onion
semisweet chocolate	plain chocolate
skillet	frying pan
tomato purée	sieved tomatoes or pasatta
unsweetened chocolate	bitter chocolat pâtissier
vanilla bean	vanilla pod
wax paper	greaseproof paper
whole milk	homogenized milk

Volume Equivalents

These are not exact equivalents for the American cups and spoons, but have been rounded up or down slightly to make measuring easier.

AMERICAN MEASURES	METRIC	IMPERIAL
¼ teaspoon	1.25 ml spoon	
½ teaspoon	2.5 ml spoon	
1 teaspoon	5 ml spoon	
½ tablespoon (1½ teaspoons)	7.5 ml spoon	
1 tablespoon (3 teaspoons)	15 ml spoon	
¼ cup (4 tablespoons)	60ml	2floz
⅓ cup (5 tablespoons)	75ml	2½floz
½ cup (8 tablespoons)	125ml	4floz
⅔ cup (10 tablespoons)	150ml	5floz (¼ pint)
¾ cup (12 tablespoons)	175ml	6floz
1 cup (16 tablespoons)	250ml	8floz
1¼ cups	300ml	10floz (½ pint)
1½ cups	350ml	12floz
1 pint (2 cups)	500ml	16floz
1 quart (4 cups)	1 litre	1¾ pints

Oven Temperatures

In the recipes in this book, only Fahrenheit temperatures have been given. Consult this chart for the Centigrade and gas mark equivalents.

OVEN	°F	°C	GAS MARK
very cool	250–275	130–140	½–1
cool	300	150	2
warm	325	170	3
moderate	350	180	4
moderately hot	375	190	5
	400	200	6
hot	425	220	7
very hot	450	230	8
	475	250	9

WEIGHT EQUIVALENTS

The metric weights given in this chart are not exact equivalents, but have been rounded up or down slightly to make measuring easier.

Avoirdupois	Metric	Avoirdupois	Metric
¼oz	7g	12oz	350g
½oz	15g	13oz	375g
1oz	30g	14oz	400g
2oz	60g	15oz	425g
3oz	90g	1lb	450g
4oz	115g	1lb 2oz	500g
5oz	150g	1½lb	750g
6oz	175g	2lb	900g
7oz	200g	2¼lb	1kg
8oz (½lb)	225g	3lb	1.4kg
9oz	250g	4lb	1.8kg
10oz	300g	4½lb	2kg
11oz	325g		

LENGTH EQUIVALENTS

The metric measurements given in this chart are not exact equivalents, but have been rounded up or down slightly to make measuring easier.

	Metric		Metric
¼ inch	5mm	2 inches	5cm
½ inch	1cm	4 inches	10cm
¾ inch	2cm	8 inches	20cm
1 inch	2.5cm	1 foot	30cm

INDEX

Designed by Paul Zakris

*Composed in Bulmer
by Trufont Typographers, Inc.,
Hicksville, New York*

*Printed and bound by Toppan Printing Company, Ltd.
Tokyo, Japan*